Chambers

professional presentations

Chambers

CHAMBERS
An imprint of Chambers Harrap Publishers Ltd
7 Hopetoun Crescent
Edinburgh EH7 4AY

First published by Chambers Harrap Publishers Ltd 2006
© Chambers Harrap Publishers Ltd 2006

A CIP catalogue record for this book is available from the British Library.

ISBN-13: 978 0550 10242 3
ISBN-10: 0550 10242 6

Designed and typeset by Chambers Harrap Publishers Ltd, Edinburgh
Printed and bound in Spain by GraphyCems

CONTRIBUTORS

Text
Rob Dazely

Editors
Sheila Ferguson
Mary O'Neill

Publishing Manager
Patrick White

Prepress Controller
Isla MacLean

Prepress Manager
Clair Simpson

CONTENTS

Introduction

Public speaking

The ability to speak really effectively to audiences is a learned skill. Good speakers are made, not born. All the great speakers of history – Winston Churchill, Martin Luther King, John F Kennedy and others – had to learn to speak well in public and knew they had to keep their skills honed. With the aid of this book, you too can learn to speak effectively in public.

In the beginning, public speaking can prove nerve-racking and you may not feel in control because there is so much to remember, but if you learn the correct techniques you will become more proficient and will, in time, come to enjoy it. This book focuses on teaching you what you need to know to help you to become a more skilful public speaker and to turn what, at present, may be an unpleasant experience into one that is pleasurable.

Who is the book aimed at?

Throughout this book reference is made both to 'talks' and 'presentations'. These expressions cover all types of public speaking, from training talks conveying information, to conference speeches involving large audiences, as well as less formal occasions such as after-dinner talks or wedding speeches. The techniques covered by the book are applicable to all types of presentation or talk, regardless of audience size.

You will find the book useful whether you are unused to making presentations or are simply seeking ways to improve your presentation skills. It is aimed both at the complete beginner and at the more experienced speaker.

The book is divided into three main parts. A checklist of items to remember is given, where appropriate, at the end of the different subsections.

Part One: Before the Talk

Part One deals with the issues you need to consider before a talk. It looks at how to deal with nerves and goes on to examine the five Ws – when, where, who, why and what. It finishes with a detailed look at talk preparation, including the use of cue cards, and the structure of the talk from the effective opening to the effective ending.

Part Two: During the Talk

The second part of the book covers everything you need to take account of during the talk, including issues such as body language, use of the voice, visual aids, what to wear, how to reduce irritating mannerisms and how to keep within a set time.

Part Three: Types of Presentation

The final section deals with the specialized techniques you need for different presentations, from complex training sessions to after-dinner talks.

You will find that by reading this book, and using the simple advice and rules it provides, your presentations will improve dramatically. We hope that public speaking will cease to terrify you and will, instead, become a positive experience.

Part One

Before the Talk

Dealing with nerves

Nerves are one of the biggest hurdles facing most speakers.

If you suffer from nerves when you are about to speak in public you are in good company. Research has shown that people are anxious about a variety of things: spiders, or snakes, or flying in aeroplanes. However, what often comes top of the list is 'public speaking'. People would rather fly in an aircraft full of spiders and snakes than get up in front of a few people and give a talk. Why?

Why do we get nervous?

We get nervous for all sorts of reasons. Firstly we feel we are being judged. We may have the following anxieties:

> *Do they think I'm competent – that I know my subject?*
>
> *Do they think I'm a good speaker?*
>
> *Do they think I'm intelligent?*
>
> *Do they think I'm attractive?*

We are also worried that we might make a fool of ourselves.

Finally we are extremely conscious of becoming the centre of attention; we notice that as we start to speak everybody is look-ing at us. This concern may have its roots in a primitive fear. In most species of apes and monkeys the stare, particularly from strangers, is a threat display.

DEALING WITH NERVES

So it is hardly surprising that we get nervous when we speak in public. We are receiving a primitive threat display from a lot of intimidating strangers and at the same time we are overly concerned about what they think of us.

'What does this audience think of me?' is an egocentric feeling rooted in our understandable concern about ourselves. However, if we allow this concern to dominate our minds we will end up thinking about ourselves rather than thinking about our audience.

It is our audience we need to concentrate on, and there are a large number of practical details to consider. These include the following questions:

- Am I speaking loudly enough?
- Am I speaking in a monotone?
- Am I looking at my audience?
- Am I moving about too much?
- Are my visual aids large enough to be seen from the back of the room?
- Is where I'm standing obscuring my visual aids?
- Am I using jargon or words they won't understand?
- Am I using terminology they might find offensive?
- Is my talk logical: does it make sense?
- Is my talk structured effectively: divided into recognizable points, with an effective opening and ending?
- Am I providing summaries during the talk to remind my audience of what I have told them?

Think about your audience and what they need, rather than thinking about yourself.

There is no magic wand. This book cannot remove your nervousness about public speaking, but what it can do is explain what preparations you need to make and what actions you need to perform in order to become an effective public speaker. Concentrate on the preparation and actions. They are the things you need to do to help your audience obtain the most benefit from your talk.

In other words, you need to make your nerves constructive. You must focus on the things that will help your audience, rather than on futile, unconstructive worry about yourself and how you appear to others.

Reducing nerves

Apart from thinking about the needs of your audience in order to make your nerves more constructive, there are however a number of techniques you can use that may help to reduce your nerves. Here are seven of the most practical ideas:

1. Be yourself

In public speaking, as in other things in life, you should never try to be something you are not.

Many people do exactly that when they get up to speak. They tell jokes, which, unless it is something they can do naturally, come out as strained and embarrassing. If they are particularly inept or insensitive they may even offend their audience.

Sometimes speakers feel they need to use long, abstruse words; language they would never normally employ. As a result they appear stilted and pretentious.

Try to imagine you are talking to a group of friends – be yourself. Use your normal language, because if you put on an act you will feel uncomfortable. Your audience will quickly pick up on your lack of belief and will find it difficult to take in what you are saying.

The only exception to the rule of being yourself is the use of swearing and jargon. Avoid both. Bad language may offend and jargon may not be understood. In both cases the audience will stop listening to you.

2. Limit your worry

You can worry about the weather but it will not make any difference to the weather. You can worry about the fact that it is Monday but it will still be Monday. You can worry about who is going to be in the audience for your presentation but (unless you can control access) people will arrive, or not, irrespective of your feelings.

In other words, there is only any point in worrying about matters that you can affect. For example, if you are worried about the amount of preparation you have done towards your presentation that is something you could (and should) do something about.

If you really cannot stop indulging in unproductive worry, then try this:

Choose a particular time of day, the time that is best for you, say from 4.30 to 5pm for example. Do not allow yourself to worry outside this period: save it up. At 4.30 find a place that you do not normally associate with work or relaxation, switch off your phone and ensure that you will be free from interruptions. When you are ready, start to allow yourself to worry about all the stuff you have resolutely shut out of your mind for the rest of the day. Try to use the time constructively to work through your problems. Have a pen and paper to hand and, if possible, come up with solutions for at least some of the issues that are worrying you.

After a few weeks of this you might recognize the pointlessness of unfocused worry. If not, at least you might have come up with some workable solutions and prevented your worry from affect-ing the rest of your day.

3. Get information

The more information you can get about the presentation you are to carry out, the better. As well as the subject itself and your time allocation, gather information on the room and equipment avail-able, the likely audience and whether or not there are other speakers.

You may not use all the information you accumulate about the subject you are speaking on, and in fact it is better if you use only a limited amount, but having the information will give you con-fidence, particularly if there are people in the audience whom you feel are experts.

4. Practise

The champion golfer Gary Player was asked after a tournament victory whether he thought the win had been lucky. 'Maybe,' he said, 'but it's funny – the harder I practise the luckier I get.'

It is exactly the same with public speaking. The more you prac-tise the better you will be. You need to practise your talk out loud. This has several advantages:

- It means that the occasion on which your audience hears the presentation is not the first time you have heard it. This will help to reduce your nerves.
- It allows you the opportunity to time the talk accurately and tells you whether you have too much, or too little, material for the time available.
- You will know in advance whether there are certain phrases which do not fit well together, or if there are words which you are unable to pronounce.

- It will highlight those areas about which you feel less than confident and prompt you to carry out further research.
- Finally, and most importantly, it gives you the chance to get feedback from a person, or people, whose opinion you trust before you have to do the talk for real. If you feel brave enough they can even video you so that you can also work on your body language. Do not do this, however, unless you feel reasonably confident. It can be a shock seeing yourself on screen for the first time and may therefore prove counterproductive.

5. Eat a high-carbohydrate snack

Public speaking takes energy and carbohydrates provide a slow energy release for the duration of the talk, so take a snack about 30 minutes beforehand. Some people also believe that carbohydrates slightly inhibit the production of adrenaline, the 'fight or flight' hormone that contributes to us feeling nervous.

6. Get to the venue early

Get to the venue at least half an hour before your audience. If you are the only speaker try to lay out the chairs and equipment in a way that suits you. The audience is then coming on to your territory, not the other way round. You also have an opportunity to check that the equipment works.

Greet as many members of the audience as you can individually as they enter the room, talk to them about trivia – their journey, the state of the weather, anything. It will calm your nerves as you wait for the start of the presentation and you will begin to see your audience as individual human beings, not as a collection of threatening strangers.

7. Use relaxation and/or visualization techniques

You need to try to relax before a big talk. Some people use physical exercise, others meditation. Use whatever technique suits you best, except alcohol or other drugs. While those substances may calm nerves, they will also adversely affect your performance – a fact that you will probably be the last to recognize.

Visualization

Visualization does not completely vanquish all the nerves but it does make you feel more positive about the presentation. Here is how it works in six steps:

Step 1

Think back to a scenario when you performed really well. It does not have to be an experience involving a public presentation although if it is, that could be a positive, powerful and useful image.

It could be an academic or sporting success, or a really significant piece of work which you performed well and for which you received justified praise from someone whose opinion you respect. It might have been a difficult situation between friends that you adroitly defused. It could be the start of a beautiful friendship; the period you realized that you had really connected with a new person.

Step 2

Run through the situation again picturing how you looked, what you wore, what you said and did. Recall feelings: what emotions and physical sensations were associated with that positive experience in your life?

Step 3

Check whether you are an observer, watching your confident, successful self, or whether you are present playing the role again.

Step 4

If you are looking at yourself from the outside, try bringing the picture closer, and put some life and colour into it.

Step 5

When you are close enough, step into it, relive it.

Step 6

Do this a few times; go in and come out again. Train yourself to do it at will and gradually you will find that you can access the feelings of control and confidence without having to go through the whole visualization process beforehand.

An experienced public speaker, who frequently has to give speeches to large audiences, regularly visualizes the time when he was best man at his brother's wedding to help calm his nerves before he speaks. He has done this so often that just using quick flashes of the memory he describes here helps to calm him.

'It was one of those times when everything "clicks". As I concentrate on the images of the wedding I am able to transport myself back to that time and that place …

I remember looking out at the wedding guests, most of whom I knew and loved. The speech seemed to hit the right tone. They laughed at the jokes and responded appropriately to the serious passages. The content and timing felt right and I found giving the speech a thoroughly pleasurable experience.

After it was over many people, among them my brother and his new wife, said how much they had loved it. That completed my enjoyment of the whole day, which I remember as a wonderful time in all our lives.'

Before he goes on stage to give a crucial speech, if he is questioning his confidence and competence and the nerves are beginning to bite, he visualizes his performance during that best man's speech and thinks to himself, 'Yes, I can do this.'

Most of us can recall situations in our lives about which we feel extremely positive. Choose one – it does not have to be a public-speaking experience – and use it regularly. It will not perform miracles, your nerves will not completely vanish, but it can calm you down and make you feel better about yourself and the talk facing you.

Checklist

1. **Use your nerves constructively**
   - to concentrate on the needs of your audience rather than on yourself

2. **Be yourself**
   - do not try to be somebody you are not

3. **Limit your worry**
   - to the things that you can do something about

4. **Get information**
   - about the subject, the room, the equipment, the audience and the other speakers

5. **Practise**
   - out loud and to a trusted audience, and get feedback on your performance and timing

6. **Eat a high-carbohydrate snack**
   - about 30 minutes before your talk

7. **Use relaxation and visualization techniques**
   - whatever works for you (but not alcohol or drugs)

The five Ws

The five Ws are:

when, where, who, why and *what*

They are useful in helping you to remember the issues you must consider before giving a talk:

- When will you be speaking and for how long?
- Where will you be speaking and what equipment do you require?
- Who will you be speaking to and how many will be present?
- Why are you speaking – what is the objective of your talk?
- What are you going to say and how will you prepare the content?

When

Check that the date you have been asked to speak is the correct one. Confirm that the day and date match up and that there have been no careless errors.

Clarify the length of time you are expected to speak. The average attention span of adults is approximately 20 minutes (much less for children or young people). This means that every 20 minutes, at the maximum, you should be quiet. Break the talk into segments, each one of which should last 20 minutes, preferably less. Either finish the talk after 20 minutes or ask your audience questions, or canvass their views. If you are speaking on a training course, set them an exercise to get them talking.

The use of case studies and exercises is explored in depth in the section on training seminars in Part Three.

Note that the audience's attention tends to be high at the beginning of a presentation, low in the middle and rises again towards the end. Structure your talk, and any exercises you provide for the audience, accordingly.

Beware of what is often called the 'graveyard slot' directly following the lunch break. At this time your audience will be digesting their food. In relative terms the blood supply to their brain reduces and increases in their digestive systems. The oxygen supply to the brain, carried in the blood, also decreases in volume to some extent. As a result they feel tired and less capable of sustained concentration.

Speakers, however animated and enthusiastic they are, may find some of their audience nodding with tiredness. In these circumstances audiences are less likely to be attentive and in the worse cases a few individuals may even drop off to sleep. Clearly none of this is in your best interests as a presenter, and experienced speakers try their best to avoid being placed in the 'graveyard slot'.

If it is unavoidable it is best to get your audience doing an exercise or working through a case study. Get them working and talking: keep your presenting to a minimum for the hour or so following lunch.

Where

It is vital to have clear directions to the venue and room in which you are speaking. If you have not received these directions at least a week before the presentation, contact the organizers.

THE FIVE WS

It is equally important to be clear about the equipment that is available in the room.

If you need a projector, computer and screen to show PowerPoint slides, or a flip chart plus paper and pens, or TV and video recorder, or any other equipment, you must ask for it in advance. To be on the safe side it is better to request it in writing, and telephone the day before to check that everything you require will be available.

So many speakers make assumptions about equipment and are then horrified when they find their assumptions are not realized. The people organizing your talk will not know what you require unless you ask for it. It is also bad practice to turn up at the allotted time and then demand a particular piece of equipment. As well as your demand making you appear unprofessional, the equipment may not be available at such short notice.

It is in your interests to take proper responsibility for ordering and checking on equipment.

If a vital piece of kit is missing, the audience will blame the person standing in front of them, ie you, not the organizers. You will also be the one that has to cope during the presentation with the problems caused by its absence.

The common types of equipment used for public speaking are:

- Screen
- Computer
- Data projector (for showing PowerPoint) with remote control
- Laser pointer or pointer
- Microphone and speakers
- Lectern
- Flip chart with paper and pens

- Overhead projector and slides (more often being replaced by PowerPoint)
- Slide projector
- TV monitor with remote control
- Back projector with large screen (at conferences)
- Video or CD player with remote control
- Video camera and stand
- Whiteboard with pens
- Blu-tak, sticky tape or wall magnets for fixing items to the wall
- Post-it notes
- Visualizer – which shows pages from books and also the presenter writing in real time

Do not forget to e-mail your PowerPoint presentation to the organizers before the talk. Alternatively, take it with you on a memory stick, CD or floppy disc (ask the organizers which is appropriate).

Arrive early, check the equipment and run through your visual aids.

Who

Analyse your audience.

You need to know how many people will be present: you would use slightly different techniques with an audience of five as opposed to one of five hundred.

It is off-putting to expect a small number and then arrive at the venue to find the large room in which you are expected to speak, quickly filling up. The reverse is also true. If you are expecting a large number and only four or five people turn up, you will feel slightly foolish and your confidence may drain away.

It is also important to be aware of the audience's level of knowledge. You need to be clear in your own mind about the following issues:

> *Which items do they particularly want you to cover?*
>
> *How much time do they have available to listen?*
>
> *Are there any remarks or subjects they may resent or find difficult?*
>
> *What do they want from the talk?*

If appropriate and practicable, issue a pre-talk questionnaire to establish what they already know, and to what level. However, this would need to be done some time in advance to enable you to tailor or extend the elements of your talk accordingly.

Example of a pre-talk questionnaire

1. Do the attached objectives for the talk meet your needs? Please circle appropriate answer.

   YES/NO

2. If 'no', what would you like to see included?

3. What, if anything, do you feel could be excluded?

4. What do you consider to be your level of knowledge of this subject area? Please tick one level.

   NO KNOWLEDGE

   BASIC

   MEDIUM

   ADVANCED

Why

Why are you doing this talk? The answer is often 'Because my boss told me I should.' Whatever your overriding reason, it is important to recognize that once you are committed to the talk you need to have a clear objective.

The objective should be expressed in terms of what your audience should feel, think, do or understand when you have finished speaking. You do not have to tell your audience your objective but you must be clear what it is. It is therefore best to write it down and refine it until you are happy.

The objective should be SMART:

Specific
Measurable
Achievable
Relevant
Time-limited

You can measure whether or not the objective of the talk has been achieved by asking the audience about the points covered in your objective breakdown. If they give the correct, relevant answers your talk has succeeded: if not, you still have some work to do. You must be able to achieve your objective in the time you have been given for the duration of the presentation.

Let's look at an example:

The tale of two objectives

Talk on Welfare Benefits

Objective 1:

> ✗ *'By the end of this talk the audience will know more about welfare benefits.'*

This objective is far too imprecise to ensure that the talk is properly focused and structured. You could fulfil the objective by telling the audience:

'Welfare benefits are benefits which come directly or indirectly from government.'

That would achieve your objective, but your audience would not have received any meaningful information.

Objective 2:

> ✔ *'By the end of this talk the audience will know:*
> *The benefits to which they are entitled;*
> *How to claim those benefits;*
> *What to do if their claim is unsuccessful.'*

This objective is specific – it states exactly what you are trying to achieve.

It is measurable – at the end of the talk you can discover whether or not it has been successful, by questioning your audience on the specific points in your objective and monitoring their answers.

It is achievable and relevant to the subject under discussion. You need to ensure that it is time-limited to the period available for the talk.

Objective 2 is more likely to lead to a structured, more focused and useful talk.

What

You know when and where you are to speak, who will be there and why you are giving the talk: you now have to decide what to say.

How to prepare and structure your talk is discussed in detail in the chapters that follow.

Checklist

1. **When**
   - check the day and the date
   - clarify how long you are expected to speak
   - try to stop after 20 minutes or break the talk into segments

2. **Where**
   - get clear directions to the venue
   - order the equipment you need in good time

3. **Who**
   - find out as much as you can about the audience
   - find out how many people will be there
   - gauge their level of knowledge about your subject

4. **Why**
   - construct a clear objective, based on what your audience should feel, think, do or understand when you finish speaking

5. **What**
   - decide what you are going to say and prepare fully for the talk

---

Talk preparation

To give an effective talk you must be properly prepared. There are five phases of preparation:

1. Identifying objective and audience
2. Researching
3. Editing
4. Applying logic
5. Practising

1. Identifying objective and audience

Firstly, as discussed earlier, you need a clear objective and a clear picture of your audience.

2. Researching

Next, collect all the material that you can on your subject. Make sure that you include everything you think might be relevant from your knowledge and your research.

You will probably fail to use a significant proportion of the material you gather from your research; in fact it is better if this is the case. You will gain confidence from the fact that your presentation is underpinned by a greater degree of knowledge of your subject.

If you are asked questions at the end of your presentation you will be in a better position to give the correct answer – or at least to guide your questioner in the right direction.

3. Editing

Now, with both the objective and the audience in mind, divide the material into three categories:

- Essential to achieve the objective
- Important to achieve the objective
- Nice for the audience to know

If you were to give the talk out loud at this stage it would almost certainly last far longer than the time available. In order to stick to the set time you need to cut most of the 'nice to know' items, plus some of the important points. You must not cut any of the essential material.

It is important to understand that what you leave out of the talk is almost as important as the information you include. You must allow time for repetition of the essential points and time to illustrate points using stories where appropriate.

4. Applying logic

Finally, organize the material logically. Do not flit from topic to topic, or from one period to another, or from a particular level of knowledge to another. If you do so, the audience will find it difficult to follow your talk and remember what you have said. Structuring your talk logically will aid, and may even speed up, your preparation.

Organize the material into a logical order by using one or more of the methods in the list below.

- **Chronological**
  Start at the beginning of the story and work through to the end.

For example, if you were telling the story of your life the obvious place to begin would be with your birth, continuing with your early life, schooling, and employment history up to the present day. You would include whatever personal information you wanted to tell people about your family, relationships, health and leisure activities in the proper order.

You would be unwise to start with:

✗ *'I went to university in Leeds, I got married in 1994, I went to school in Manchester, I was born in Huddersfield and I like cinema and reading biographies.'*

People would simply be unable to follow the thread of your presentation.

- **Topic area**
  Finish one topic area before you move on to the next. For example:

If you were doing a talk on cooking a special dish you would probably start with the ingredients, follow with the cooking instructions and finish with tips on presentation of the meal.

A talk on a foreign holiday might start with the planning of the holiday, the culture and language of the country and, finally, the attractions you visited when you arrived at your destination.

A presentation on a sport, or game, may start with the history of the game, move on to the rules of the game and finish with a brief summary of the specific skills necessary to play the game.

- **Level of audience knowledge**

  Try to find out what your audience knows before preparing your talk.

  If you have an audience with a mixed ability level, plan your talk to start at the lowest level, moving quickly, with clear explanations, to more complex concepts.

  Speakers worry that the higher-ability people may become bored if they do this, and clearly that is possible. However, the likelihood of boredom is reduced if you explain what you are doing, and do not spend too long on the basics. Indeed, even some of the high-fliers may find a reminder of first principles extremely useful.

  If you start at the middle level, those that know little about the subject will probably struggle to understand your talk and are likely to lose interest quickly. The result will be that the talk is a waste of time for a significant part of your audience – not an ideal situation for a public speaker.

5. Practising

Practising the talk assists you to become more familiar with the subject. It also ensures that the first time you actually speak the words is not in front of your audience.

When you have edited the talk as much as you think is necessary, and have put your points in a logical order, practise the talk out loud, timing it carefully. Allow extra time for presenting your visual aids.

If the presentation is still too long you need to cut some more of your material. Remember not to cut any of the essential points.

TALK PREPARATION

Do not try to fit your talk into the set time by speeding up or rushing through important points: you will only confuse your audience.

The next task is to structure the talk. This is based on the three golden rules of public speaking:

1. **Tell them what you are going to tell them**
2. **Tell them**
3. **Tell them what you have told them**

The typical talk structure is as follows:

```
Effective opening
        ⇩
Outline of the main points
        ⇩
Main points (1, 2, 3, etc)
        ⇩
Interim summing-up (after each main point)
        ⇩
Summary
        ⇩
Effective ending
```

Effective opening

The opening of a presentation is very important. This is the period when the audience makes a judgement on whether or not you are likely to be a good speaker. If you make a weak opening it takes time to correct the poor first impression and occasionally you never manage to do so. Alternatively, a good opening can create real appreciation within your audience that will be sustained well into the talk.

Unfortunately, many speakers start badly. They do not appear to be ready for their audience or they apologize for not preparing properly.

If you were going into an operation and the surgeon said to you, 'Sorry, I haven't really prepared for this ...' it would not fill you with confidence. Do not start your talk with an apology or your audience will experience similar misgivings.

Sometimes speakers apologize to lower the expectations of the audience or excuse their own shortcomings. Sometimes they apologize because they genuinely have not prepared. If this is the case, then there is no point in you being there: it is impossible to give an effective talk without proper preparation.

Whatever the reason, an apology creates a bad first impression.

Stand up at the start of your presentation and wait for silence. It is far better to stand, rather than give your talk from a seated position. It is important that you stand up whatever the size of your audience, but it is vital if you have a large audience. If you stand your listeners can see you and, equally importantly, you can see them.

In an upright position your voice will be projected out to hit the back wall of the room. The human body absorbs a lot of sound and if you are seated you will be projecting your voice into the people in the front row, so that listeners at the back of the room may be unable to hear you.

So stand up, look at your audience and, if you can, smile. Only do so if you can smile without giving the sort of frozen grin which will inform the audience that you are nervous.

This is the time when you are likely to be at your most anxious, so it is a good idea to learn the first few phrases of your talk by heart as you do not want to start with a hesitant 'er' or 'um'. Your opening remarks do not have to be profound or funny (although obviously it is beneficial if they are), they just have to be effective.

To get started, here are some of the basic expressions you can use to greet your audience and introduce yourself:

> *Good morning/afternoon/evening.*
>
> *Good evening ladies and gentlemen.*
>
> *Hello everybody.*

> *I was very happy to be invited to speak to you today.*
>
> *It's very nice to be here.*
>
> *I'm very pleased to be with you.*
>
> *It's a pleasure to be here today.*

> *My name's [your name] and I'm from [company name].*
>
> *I am the [your job] at [company name].*
>
> *I am [your name] and I represent [company name].*
>
> *I think you all know me.* (if giving a talk to colleagues for example)

You can merely introduce yourself and the title of your talk before moving on to the outline of the main points. However, if you feel able to do something slightly different you could make your audience think, 'This is going to be good.'

If you feel that you are holding the audience in the palm of your hand and that they cannot wait to hear what comes next, you have succeeded in your opening.

Try the following techniques:

- **Start with a personal anecdote.** Keep it short, relevant and non-offensive, and avoid questionable humour.

- **Ask a question.** If the question is not rhetorical be prepared for all possible answers and assess how you will use those answers to lead into the subject of the talk.

- **Use a visual prop.** If you are talking about something physical, and it is possible to bring the item safely and easily into the room, it can make an effective opening. Sometimes getting the audience to use their imagination is enough. Note the example, outlined below, of the miner – he was unable to show the audience his workspace but created a picture in their minds by using the speaker's table.

- **Mention something relevant to your audience.** This could be, for example, the difficulty in getting to the venue, a problem they have probably also encountered, or the appalling train service or roadworks (either of which is usually a safe bet).

- **Do something unusual.** A speaker on assertiveness once started his talk by ignoring the audience and sitting down with his feet on the desk, reading a newspaper in silence. After a few minutes he opened by saying: 'Nobody asked me what I was up to for the last five minutes: you lot really need this talk!'

  Do think carefully though before using a technique like this. It can backfire unless it is handled well, or if you do not get the expected reaction.

Examples of excellent openings

- The radical politician whose opening remarks to a staid, complacent audience were:

    'Good afternoon. I represent the end of the world as you know it.'

- The coalminer who, at the beginning of his talk, pointed to the 2m × 1m space beneath the speaker's table and said:

    'Look at this space. How big do you think it is?' (he waited for answers) 'Now, imagine yourself in this space. I work in an area no bigger than this, eight hours a day.'

- The management guru who started her speech with:

    'Management is like a tea bag. You don't know how good it is until it gets into hot water.'

- The best man who began his speech:

    'As you know, most best man speeches concern tales of drunkenness, debauchery and detoxification. Unfortunately I can't just concentrate on the bride, I have to talk about the groom as well.'

Outline of the main points

This is the part where you 'tell them what you are going to tell them'. You should inform the audience of the points you will cover in your talk. Some phrases you could use to introduce the outline are:

I've divided my talk into four parts.

My talk will focus on three main areas.

In the first part I will look at …

The second part will deal with ...

In the final part I'll show you ...

It is far more effective if you have a slide showing the points clearly. Try to keep the titles of the points brief and concise so that the audience will remember them more easily.

For example, if you were doing a presentation introducing an audience to management techniques your outline might be:

- Leadership styles
- Communication
- Motivation
- Delegation
- Dealing with poor performance
- Staff development

An outline of a presentation on a holiday venue might include:

- How to get there
- Places to stay
- Language
- Culture
- Attractions
- Precautions

Main points

This is where you 'tell them'. The main points cover the essential subjects of your talk. You might introduce your first main point with:

I'd like to start now by looking at ...

In this first part of my presentation I want to look at ...

Firstly, I'd like to consider ...

> *To begin with, I'm going to review …*

When moving on to subsequent points, you could say:

> *Moving on now to my next point: [title of point].*
> *Now I'd like to look at …*
> *Let's turn now to …*

Each time you start a main point it is a good idea to show the title of the point on a slide. All the main points are equally import-ant and should be approximately equal in length.

Main points may be subdivided. For example, a main point enti-tled 'modes of travel' could be divided into:

- Walking
- Bicycles
- Boats
- Trains
- Buses
- Planes

Interim summing-up

The interim summing-up is part of telling the audience what you have told them. It is carried out after each main point. There is no need go over the details of the point again, unless it is a partic-ularly long or complicated one. All you need to do is inform the audience that the point is completed and now you are moving on to the next one. Use your slides to emphasize the move from one point to the next.

You need to give the audience a 'box' of information. Telling them you are about to cover the point is opening the box. By covering the point you are giving the audience the contents of the box. The interim summing-up closes that particular box and opens the next one. Information provided in this way is easier to remember.

If you give someone a page full of numbers, then take the page away and ask them to recall as many numbers as possible, most people will remember more numbers if they are grouped into three boxes or tables. It helps if there is approximately the same amount of numbers in each box. In the same way it helps if you 'box' or structure your information during a talk, with approximately the same amount of information in each section.

You are also letting your audience know where they are in the talk. Occasionally, telling them that you have finished a point, and that you are moving on to the next, may reclaim wandering attention.

Summary

The summary is the final part of telling the audience what you have told them. You could introduce your summary by saying, for example:

> *So, what we have looked at here today is …*
>
> *I'd like to end now by summarizing the main points of my talk.*

During the summary you do not have to go over the material again, even in an abbreviated form. It is sufficient to tell the audience briefly that you have covered the points. It is better if you show a slide at this juncture, which should be a duplicate of the outline slide you used at the beginning of the talk. Employ exactly the same titles for the points you have covered: the summary should have no new information. It simply completes the task of 'telling them what you have told them' and preparing the audience for the end of the talk.

Effective ending

Speakers often spoil a good presentation with a poor ending. They will sometimes say '… and finally', and continue speaking for ten minutes and then repeat '… and finally' once or twice before eventually ending the presentation. The other common fault is to finish too abruptly, taking the audience by surprise.

You should know how you are going to finish a talk before you stand up to begin. The words you use at the end of the talk are the last thing the audience will hear, so the ending should leave them with a good impression.

The final phrases should be brief but your audience should be in no doubt that you have finished. It can be as simple as:

> *That's all I have to say about this subject for now.*
>
> *Thank you very much for your attention.*
>
> *I'd like to end now by thanking you for your attention.*
>
> *Thank you for listening, are there any questions?*

Alternatively you might say something humorous, or profound, or perhaps try a call to action. Whatever you decide, keep it brief and then be quiet.

Checklist

1. **Effective opening**
- rehearse your opening
- wait for silence
- look at your audience and smile
- open without apology or hesitation

2. **Outline of the main points**
    - tell your audience what you are going to cover
    - show them a slide outlining your points
    - keep it simple

3. **Main points**
    - show the title of each point on a slide
    - keep the points approximately equal in length

4. **Interim summing-up**
    - 'close the box', ie close off each main point before telling the audience you are moving on to the next

5. **Summary**
    - show the audience the points you have covered in your talk by using a duplicate of the slide used to outline the main points.

6. **Effective ending**
    - know how you are going to end before you start the talk
    - make the planned ending brief and then be quiet

Use of cue cards

Some speakers try to learn their talk parrot-fashion. Although knowing a talk well is obviously a good thing, and learning bits of it by heart, such as the opening, is helpful, learning the whole talk by rote is not recommended. It will sound like a stilted recital rather than a natural, live performance with a few acceptable rough edges. Moreover, if interruptions occur, which invariably happens, it can mean the thread of an over-rehearsed speech is lost.

Reading the talk is unacceptable. You will lose eye contact with your audience while you do so and it will sound unnatural: in fact, just as though you were reading it. Reading a script and sounding spontaneous is an art that very few people possess.

So, unless you have given the same talk many times, it is likely you will have to use notes.

You will see speakers using their visual aids as notes. The problem with this technique, apart from using far too many slides, is that the speaker ends up looking at the screen (or, if using PowerPoint, their computer) a great deal. This again results in a loss of eye contact with the audience which, as will be discussed in Part Two, 'Body language', is a loss to be avoided at all costs.

Using a sheet, or sheets, of A4 paper for your notes can give away the fact that you are nervous; the movement of the paper will accentuate the tremor of a shaky hand.

USE OF CUE CARDS

If you decide to use a pad of A4 to reduce this movement then the pad becomes a noticeable item which can create a slight barrier between you and your audience.

The solution is cue cards. These are small, flexible cards – approximately 10cm x 6cm in size – that can fit in the palm of the hand. The cards should be numbered, and fastened together by threading a treasury tag (a short piece of string with a small length of metal at each end) through a punched hole in one corner. The length of the string allows the cards to be turned over easily.

If the cards are accidentally spilled on to the floor, failure to connect them in this way may result in a talk being delivered in an extremely random order.

You should put one point on each card. These are not just the 'main points' but all the points you want to say on the subject. Keep the words you use on the cards to a minimum so you will not be tempted to read them rather than look at your audience. By the time you come to give your talk you should know your subject so well that each card should prompt a flow of information. This will make your delivery more natural and less stilted than reading from detailed notes.

The cards do not provide a script. They 'cue' you to give information in a logical order, and stop you from wandering from the subject. They can also, among other things, remind you to show a visual aid, provide a summary, carry out an exercise or even help with the timing of your talk.

As you deal with the point on a card, turn the card over and move on to the next one.

Tips for timing

- Ensure that you have 'essential', 'important' and 'nice to know' points scattered throughout the cue cards.

- Underline each category in a different colour – for example, red for 'essential', blue for 'important' and green for 'nice to know'.

- If you are running short of time and you come to a 'green' card simply turn it over, without mentioning the information it cues you to give. You can even do this with the 'blue' cards, but you *must* cover the information on the 'red' cards.

- If you are comfortably within time, include all the cards.

You can also use the cards to prompt you to 'slow down', show a slide, or involve the audience in some way – perhaps by asking questions or setting an exercise.

As you deliver your talk hold the cards in one hand, turning them over using your other hand after you have made the point written on the card. This also has the advantage of dealing with the dilemma of what to do with your hands during a talk.

Hold the cards at chest level. Look at your audience most of the time; only look down occasionally to check what is on your cards.

Checklist

1. Use small, flexible, numbered cards fastened together with treasury tags

2. Write one point per card
- keep the writing brief to 'cue' your memory

USE OF CUE CARDS

3. **Underline the cards in a different colour depending on their category of importance**
- use the colours to remind yourself to ignore, or include, less important cards depending on the amount of time available

4. **Prompt yourself by using appropriate cards**
- to slow down
- to show a slide
- to involve the audience

5. **Look mostly at your audience, not at your cards**

Part Two

During the Talk

The important elements of communication

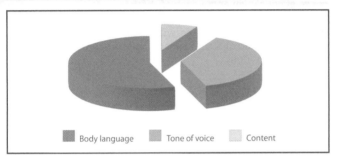

Body language | Tone of voice | Content

This chart indicates that when we communicate face to face only about 7% of our message is conveyed by the words that we use (the **content**). The **tone of voice** accounts for 38% and our posture and gestures, or **body language**, a startling 55%.

Humans are primates, a group that also contains the monkeys and apes; creatures which rely a great deal on gestures and posture to communicate. We have inherited the ability to pick up non-verbal messages from others of our kind, and do it subconsciously. Often we do not realize it is happening. This can make the percentages, shown in the chart, difficult for us to believe but does not make them any less true.

If, for example, you ask a friend who appears depressed, 'What's the matter?' and they reply 'Nothing' in a low, apathetic tone of voice, with a defensive posture and downcast gaze, then you know that something is the matter. You believe their body language and the tone of their voice rather than the content of what they are saying.

THE IMPORTANT ELEMENTS OF COMMUNICATION

When speaking in public it is clearly important that the content of your talk is factual, accurate and relevant. However, even if the content is factual and accurate, your audience will not believe you, or find your talk interesting, unless it is presented with a sense of conviction and a dash of charisma.

In other words, a talk packed with useful information will come across as dull and difficult to absorb unless you get the tone and body language right.

Body language

How you look and move about a room will have a tremendous influence on how your audience feels about you. If you look and sound confident, even if you do not feel it on the inside, people will view you as a competent speaker in control of your subject and yourself.

There are three important aspects to body language:

- Eye contact
- Hand gestures
- Stance

Eye contact

Of all the advice given in this book the next line is arguably the most important:

> **You must look at your audience while you are speaking to them.**

If you are talking to a friend, or even a casual acquaintance, you will normally maintain normal eye contact, ie look in their eyes for a few seconds, then look away briefly before looking back again. Those who fail to do this are perceived as shifty: they find it difficult to establish trust and are not so readily believed.

We know all this, yet when some people get in front of an audience they look at the screen behind them, apparently fascinated by their visual aid, which they have read and seen dozens of times previously. Occasionally speakers are captivated for the duration of their talk by the view from the nearest window. Alternatively they look at the spaces between people, or just above their heads, rather than in their eyes.

We often turn our gaze away when speaking in public because looking at the audience is frightening, particularly when you are trying to remember all of the information that you want to impart. It is also the case that the speaker has to look at many people and meet many pairs of eyes, whereas an audience member only has to look at the speaker.

The problem is that the first thing that will betray your nerves to an audience, even though they will only pick this up subconsciously, is the fact that you are not looking at them.

The good news is that there is an advantage in all this. If you can force yourself to look at the audience it will go a long way in helping you to appear competent and in control, even if this is far from the truth.

So how do you maintain eye contact with your audience?

In small groups of up to, say, twelve people, spend a couple of seconds looking each person in the eye before moving on calmly to the next. Do not flick your eyes too quickly from one person to another as that too will make you appear nervous.

Conversely, do not fix on a friendly face and stare at them. Although you may not even notice you are doing so because you are concentrating on your talk, the rest of your audience will feel ignored, and the person concerned will start to feel very uncomfortable.

In large audiences, during conference speeches for example, try this:

The five-person trick

- Choose a person at the extreme right of the front row and a person at the extreme left of the front row.

- Next, choose a person at either end of the back row. You should now have picked a person in each corner of the audience.

- Choose a person in the centre of the audience.

- Finally, move your eyes regularly from person to person, among your chosen five people, ensuring you do so at eye-level height. You will have to move your head to do this.

Every member of the audience will feel you are looking at them.

One thing you will have to get used to is that the audience may not always seem bothered whether you look at them or not. They possess the anonymity of being in a crowd and therefore do not always feel the need to appear interested.

This does not mean they are not listening. In fact, unless they are reading a newspaper or obviously asleep (in which case you should get them doing something such as an exercise, or asking questions or even taking a short break if possible), you must convince yourself they are listening.

You should do this because, even if their attention has momentarily wandered, they will almost certainly start listening again soon. This is particularly true if you say something like: 'I've finished point one, now I'm moving on to the next point.' An interim summing-up such as this can actually help you regain attention.

You also need to believe that they are interested, so as to give yourself confidence.

Maintaining eye contact can be a bit scary. You also might find it difficult to think of what you need to say next while looking at all those faces. Persevere: it does become easier with practice.

Despite any initial difficulties, eye contact with your audience is well worth the time and trouble and it confers huge advantages on a speaker.

Hand gestures

Try not to fold your arms across your chest or move them near your mouth; both these gestures are defensive and can give your audience the impression that you are unsure of the content of your talk. In addition, if you partially cover your mouth your listeners will find it difficult to hear you.

If you feel more comfortable clasping your hands, try to ensure that you are doing so quite low down, near your waist, so that you are not creating a nervous, protective barrier across the upper part of your body.

Do not point or jab your index finger at the audience as this is perceived as being aggressive.

If you hold things in your hands, other than cue cards or a pointer for your visual aid, you are likely to play with them. Speakers can become fascinated with paper clips, transforming them into all sorts of weird shapes, or else click the top of their pen repeatedly, to the extent that it drives their audience slowly mad. The audience's concentration shifts to the item in the speaker's hands, away from what the speaker is saying.

If you have pockets, only ever place one hand in them. Standing with both hands in your pockets either looks too casual or else overly defensive. Do not jingle any change you have in your pockets and try not to fidget.

All these gestures are a sign of nerves. If you consciously relax, they will disappear.

Make your hand signals calm, unambiguous and purposeful. Try to move your hands slowly and steadily rather than jerkily. Think about your hand movements: some speakers actually practise them in front of the mirror.

Remember that body language contributes a huge amount to your audience's understanding of your talk.

Stance

Stand with your legs slightly apart. You should appear relaxed rather than rigid, or 'standing to attention'.

Do not walk about too much or rock backwards and forwards. Rocking back indicates that you do not want to be here giving this talk, whereas the forward movement occurs because you realize you have to stay. To prevent yourself rocking, try to transfer most of your weight on to one foot so that the act of rocking will become far more difficult.

Body language is important because your audience always notices it. They do so subconsciously; they will not know why they perceive you as unsure and nervous, or assured and confident, but nevertheless they will interpret the signals correctly.

As a speaker you must take as much care to use appropriate body language as you do over the content of your talk.

BODY LANGUAGE

Good, assertive body language pays dividends.

1. **Look at your audience**
- scan your listeners, spending a few seconds on each person without fixing on one individual
- with larger audiences use the five-person eye-contact trick

2. **Use calm, unambiguous hand gestures**
- clasp your hands low if necessary, or hold your arms slightly away from your body, palms down
- do not fold your arms across your chest
- avoid moving your hands near your mouth or jabbing your index finger aggressively
- grasp nothing in your hands except cue cards or a pointer
- do not fidget

3. **Stand with your legs slightly apart**
- if necessary, transfer most of your weight on to one foot to prevent rocking
- do not walk about too much, or put both hands in your pockets

Use of the voice

There is a memory aid, or mnemonic, you can use to help recall the issues you should consider whilt using your voice for public speaking.

The mnemonic is VAMPS:

Volume
Articulation
Modulation & mannerisms
Pronunciation
Speed

Volume

You must be loud enough to be heard by all your audience, even those people sitting right at the back of the room.

To ensure this happens, fill your lungs to capacity, pause and count silently to three before exhalation, to prevent hyperventilation.

Now exhale the air from your lungs, silently, slowly and evenly through your mouth, before you speak.

Do not control the outflow of breath from your mouth by closing your throat. Instead use your diaphragm, the dome-shaped membrane that separates the chest from the abdomen. In other words, breathe so that your whole chest and abdomen move, rather than only your upper chest.

Repeat this a few times before you begin to speak.

This exercise ensures there is sufficient oxygen in your brain and lungs to perform the twin tasks of thinking and speaking. You will be at your most nervous at the start of your talk and nerves tend to make you breathe more rapidly and shallowly. Unless you take deep breaths your lungs could be starved of oxygen.

Nerves may also cause your mouth to be dry. It is a good idea always to have a glass of water to hand. Even if you find you do not require it, it is comforting to know that it is there.

As you begin to speak, look at your audience, direct your head towards them and try to hit the back wall of the room with your voice. If you get the opportunity to do so, practise beforehand in the room in which you plan to speak.

Exercise for volume control

- Sound a note and, without changing the pitch, gradually increase the volume.

- Control the outflow of breath by using the diaphragm.

- Continue the note as long as possible without allowing the volume to fade.

- Practise this technique often; the note will become louder and longer.

- Try it with a range of notes and eventually your voice will increase in volume.

Articulation

Do not mumble. You need to speak more accurately and clearly than you would in social conversation. Try not to swallow the ends of your words. In particular, ensure that you carefully enunciate difficult words or explanations of jargon.

Modulation

The only people who actually want to send their listeners to sleep are hypnotists. Consequently they speak in an even monotone, never raising or lowering their voice significantly. If you speak in a monotone, you too will send your listeners to sleep.

- Raise and lower the volume of your voice throughout your presentation.
- Try to speak in a lower or higher pitch from time to time.
- Use silence occasionally.
- Emphasize particularly important words or phrases by speaking more slowly.

It can be a good idea to write something like 'Watch the voice' on every tenth cue card to remind you to vary your voice, and make listening to it more interesting.

Mannerisms

The most common verbal mannerism is saying 'er ...' or 'um ...'. Some speakers constantly use the phrase 'you know' or 'ok?' at the end of sentences, or repeat words such as 'actually' or 'basically'.

These verbal tics are difficult to get rid of, but you must try to do so because they indicate that you are nervous, thereby making the audience less confident about what you are saying. Once the audience notice your verbal mannerisms they can become irritated by them or, worse, start counting them.

These mannerisms occur due to nerves and because speakers are scared of silence. They therefore put something in place of the silence. However, silence is not a bad thing. It is certainly better than 'er' or 'um', and can be used very effectively as a pause, before emphasizing points you wish your listeners to remember. Although any such pause may seem like an eternity to you, in reality it will probably only last a couple of seconds and will help your audience understand your talk more clearly.

To deal with verbal mannerisms you firstly have to realize you are using them. You can do this by getting feedback from a person you trust, as explained in Part One, 'Dealing with nerves', or you can tape yourself speaking.

Once you recognize there is a problem, you need to force yourself to use silence when you feel an 'er, um, you know', or any other mannerism, about to emerge.

At first you might sound slightly robotic but eventually your delivery will improve and the annoying verbal tics will become, if not a thing completely of the past, at least greatly reduced.

Pronunciation

Try to avoid using words you cannot pronounce easily. As you get to them in your presentation you are likely to stumble and sound unsure of yourself.

Sometimes a particular word may cause no problems on its own, but when it is grouped with others your pronunciation becomes mired in difficulties.

Writers of tongue-twisters knew this. 'She sells sea shells on the seashore' is hard to say accurately although each word on its own is easy.

The only way to discover if you have a problem with any part of your talk is to practise it out loud privately, before you deliver it to an audience. Simply remove the items that cause you difficulties.

The only exception to this is if the word or phrase is an integral part of the presentation. If you must use the word, the secret is to break up the spelling of the word phonetically (for example, think of dolphins as 'doll-fins'). Practise a few times, and the problem disappears.

Speed

Most people speak too quickly when giving a presentation. This is because they do not want to be there, and the faster they speak, the earlier they can escape. Unfortunately the audience are more than capable of picking up the fact that you are speaking too rapidly, and correctly interpret it as nerves on your part.

The solution is to practise the presentation and consciously slow down the rhythm of your speech. Assume that when you get in front of the audience you will speed up, so practise out loud (if not the whole talk then at least certain sections) several times, until you feel confident about delivering the talk in a measured manner.

You can use your cue cards to help stop yourself from talking too quickly. Write SLOW DOWN in large letters on several cards throughout the talk to remind you to do so. Try to put silences at the end of phrases or short sections.

Allow the audience time to absorb what you have just said.

Checklist

Remember VAMPS when speaking:

1. **Volume**
- speak up

2. **Articulation**
- speak carefully

3. **Modulation**
- vary the pitch of your voice
- avoid 'er' and 'um' or repeating words or phrases

4. **Pronunciation**
- avoid words you cannot pronounce; alternatively practise saying them phonetically

5. **Speed**
- slow down

Storytelling

Everyone likes stories. A main point can usually be made most effectively by giving an example from your experience.

If you plan to use a story, think about the information you receive through your five senses. The result is likely to bring the experience to life for your audience. So ask yourself:

> *How did it look?*
> *How did it taste?*
> *How did it smell?*
> *How did it sound?*
> *How did it feel?*

Think about using stories based on your personal experience of issues such as:

- **Minor crises** – trains being delayed; traffic jams; mislaying your money, passport or ticket; spills and breakages; stories about problems caused by children.

- **Significant events in your life** – the birth of a child; bereavement; illness.

- **Real-life humour** – based on daft things that have actually happened, preferably to you.

Many speakers are scared to try this. Some are worried about the story falling flat and not receiving the hoped-for reaction from the audience. In the case of those presenting scientific papers they are concerned that they will be perceived as unprofessional.

However, the stories do not need to be funny or profound; if they are it is a bonus. They are merely required to help your audience to remember what you say. The audience will do so more clearly if you can put an image in their heads that they can relate to.

So rather than say:

> *'This particular series of experiments did not produce the expected result: it was felt this was due to unexpectedly cold conditions.'*

You could try:

> *'Last November was freezing, and the heating in the laboratory failed overnight. I remember that on November 30th there was snow on the ground. I noticed how cold it **felt** as soon as I entered the laboratory, and I **saw** my breath clouding in front of my face. This was the probable cause of the result you see before you.'*

The second passage says the same thing as the first but the audience is far more likely to remember it because you have given them an image of yourself coming in through the snow to an unheated room.

To make a good impact on opening, try starting your talk with a brief story. A conference speaker started her presentation by saying:

> *'Unlike some people, I love the **taste** of broccoli. I passed the cafeteria just now and **saw** the lunch menu.*
>
> *The good news for me is that there is broccoli on the menu, straight after I finish.*

> *The good news for you is that I will make absolutely sure I do not overrun.'*

The words in bold type, in the two examples shown, emphasize how repeating your experience, through the use of words associated with the senses and the feelings, can bring a story alive for your audience.

Stories are good because they bring interest to an occasionally dull subject, but crucially they must be the right type of stories.

They must be:

- **Brief and not too numerous.** Three or four short stories in a 20-minute presentation is fine but many more than that and you can come across as a raconteur, rather than a lecturer with a weighty subject to impart. That is fine for an after-dinner speech but not so desirable if you are attempting to train people in a subject area that is unfamiliar to them.

  Keep the stories brief. Long, rambling anecdotes can lose the attention of your audience and thereby fail to emphasize the point you were attempting to reinforce.

- **Relevant.** The story should illustrate, and bring to life, a point that you are trying to make to help the audience's memory. Do not tell a story just for the sake of appearing amusing. Unless the occasion is extremely informal, jokes that you heard from a friend or read somewhere are best left for purely social occasions.

- **Non-offensive.** Under no circumstances should there be any hint of bad language, blasphemy, racism, sexism or any other stereotyping in your stories.

  Apart from the moral question you will alienate at least part, if not all, of your audience with such language. They will stop listening to you and may easily become hostile. This is the last reaction any sensible speaker wants to cause in their listeners.

If you are worried, check out the stories you are planning to use with someone whose opinion you trust, and who knows the audience to whom you will be speaking.

If in doubt, leave it out.

Your stories do not have to be bland just because you are careful in your use of language. Be creative; think how you could use a story to make a relevant point more memorable and interesting.

For example, a speaker who wanted to illustrate that people often remember more clearly what they are shown and what they smell, rather than what they hear, shared this recollection:

> *'I was at the zoo, teaching a group of students about communication in animals. We were approaching the hippopotamus enclosure when I saw the hippo, Henry, lumber up on to the bank near the enclosure fence.*
>
> *Hippos mark their territory by flicking their dung from side to side with their short tail, at approximately hippo head height. Their dung consists mainly of an evil smelling, green liquid.*
>
> *I told all the students to move back from the fence and everyone, except one person, did so.*
>
> *Henry territorially marked him from his head to his feet. The other students, as you might imagine, found this hilarious.*
>
> *Later when they sat their exams they proved they had, unfortunately, forgotten a lot of what they had been*

told. However, all of them, without exception, remem-
bered how hippos mark their territory.'

By using the storytelling technique the speaker amused and
relaxed both himself and his listeners. He also put the vision of
the location and situation in his listeners' heads and reinforced
the point he was making.

In summary, his story helped the audience to remember what he
had said.

Checklist

1. **Use stories to emphasize important points**
   - try to relate things from your own experience, using descriptive words based on the five senses

2. **Ensure you do not use too many stories**

3. **Ensure your stories are brief, relevant and non-offensive**

Language

The use of language can be examined under two main headings

- Jargon
- Appropriate language

Jargon

Audiences hate unexplained TLAs.

All that a TLA does is confuse them. While they are trying desperately to work out what your latest, unfathomable TLA means they are not listening to you.

If you constantly use TLAs, and fail to explain what they mean you will cause exactly the reaction in your listeners that you are suffering from at the moment, as you read about them.

TLAs, by the way, are Three-Letter Abbreviations, and they can prove very annoying.

As well as being confusing, jargon is elitist and irritating. It says to your audience that you feel they should know what your abbreviations or acronyms mean. It also ensures that they will fail to understand at least part of what you say.

The test of whether something is jargon is that you should be able to use your abbreviation with anyone you meet in the street. If they speak your language but still do not understand what you are talking about, you are probably using jargon.

Jargon is insidious. Because you use a number of abbreviations all the time with your work colleagues, you stop thinking of them as jargon. They become part of your ordinary speech and then you start to use them outside the workplace.

That is when you are on the road to audience confusion and annoyance.

However, abbreviations are not the only problem. Any difficult or technical word or phrase that you use should be explained at least once, and preferably reinforced by a visual aid. Or you could issue a glossary of abbreviations and technical terms as a hand-out to accompany your talk.

Appropriate language

Using the right language is not just about being careful to avoid jargon. You have to make sure the language you use is appropriate in that it will not offend members of your audience.

Slang and bad language

Although many slang words are widely understood (such as 'gob' for 'mouth', 'fag' for 'cigarette' and 'dosh' for 'money'), these produce a highly informal style when used in speech. Using them in a formal presentation would show that you did not appreciate what sort of language the situation requires.

Of course, you should avoid swearing. You are extremely likely to upset some, if not all, of your listeners. As a result they will cease to listen to you. Bad language may mean that you lose at least part of your audience; sometimes literally, as they may walk out.

Non-discriminatory terminology

You must also be meticulous about using non-discriminatory terminology. Language is most likely to be considered as offensive when it implies a judgement about other individuals or about groups to which other individuals belong, or seems to exclude them in some way.

The following subjects each present their own problems to the speaker:

- gender
- race and nationality
- physical and mental capability

In addition to these, a speaker should be careful if touching on the subjects of:

- religion
- age
- sexuality
- marital or family status
- political beliefs

Gender

You risk offending many of your audience if you use language in a way that implies that there is only one gender, or that one gender is superior to the other.

To avoid using words in ways that reinforce stereotypes about the gender roles, there are a number of things you can do:

- When talking about a person's occupation, prefer neutral terms to gender-specific terms, for example 'spokesperson' as opposed to 'spokesman' or 'spokeswoman'.

- Avoid using titles that imply that an occupation is done by only one gender. Use, for example, 'sales representative' rather than 'salesman'.

- Avoid using words ending in -ess (such as 'manageress') when referring to a woman's occupation, especially when there is a neutral alternative available.

- Avoid referring to women as though they are doing men's jobs ('a lady doctor'), or referring to men as though they are doing women's jobs ('a male nurse').

- It is usually possible to find an alternative to the word 'man' being used to refer to men and women (in phrases such as 'the benefits that science has brought to man'). You could use, for example, 'people' or 'humankind'.

Gender also presents a problem in language because the masculine pronouns 'he', 'him' and 'his' are often considered the normal forms.

> *Anyone can learn a foreign language if **he** wants to.*

Try to avoid exclusive use of masculine pronouns by using 'he or she' or 'they':

> *Anyone can learn a foreign language if **he or she** wants to.*

> *Anyone can learn a foreign language if **they** want to.*

Race and nationality

The subject of race and nationality is another area that requires sensitive treatment. It is not just a question of avoiding crude stereotypes and deliberately offensive terms.

- Be aware of appropriate terms to refer to people's race or racial origin. For example, 'Afro-Caribbean' is preferred to 'West Indian', and 'British Asian' is preferred for British citizens whose families originate from the Indian subcontinent.

LANGUAGE

- Use positive terms rather than define people by what they are not. Terms such as 'non-white' should be used only when the context makes them relevant.

- Do not describe people in ways that reinforce stereotypes about their race or nationality (for example, referring to a Chinese person as inscrutable, a German as efficient, or a Scot as thrifty).

Physical and mental capability

Some of the language used when referring to people with disabilities has associations of pity and limitation, and can cause disabled people to be seen in terms of their disability, rather than be treated as individuals. There are a number of things you can do to avoid this:

- Beware of describing people solely in terms of a disability. It is better to talk of 'a person with a disability' or 'a disabled person' rather than, for example, 'an invalid'. Similarly, it is preferable to talk about 'people with epilepsy' or 'deaf people' rather than 'epileptics' or 'the deaf'.

- Many disabled people dislike being referred to as 'handicapped' on the grounds that a handicap is created by external surroundings or by other people's attitudes, and not by the disability itself.

- It is preferable to refer to someone as 'using a wheelchair' rather than being 'confined to a wheelchair', or 'wheelchair-bound'. Similarly, it is better to say that someone has a particular disability rather than 'suffering from' or being 'afflicted by' it.

There are often differences between the ways people refer to themselves, and the ways that they like to be referred to by others. Remember that a group may use a term about itself, but might object to it when it is used by others. Also, ideas about appropriate language might vary from country to country or region to region.

You should also bear in mind that appropriate terminology changes from time to time, and terms that were once considered acceptable might now be regarded as offensive.

It is your responsibility, as the speaker, to investigate the appropriate non-discriminatory language and terminology. If you fail to use modern terminology, acceptable to your listeners, you demonstrate to them that you are out of touch and insensitive to their needs.

It is in your interests to get this important, but relatively simple, facet of your talk correct. It is you who will suffer from the displeasure and lack of concentration and respect from your audience if you get it wrong.

Checklist

1. **Avoid jargon**
   - if you use abbreviations or technical terms you must explain them

2. **Use appropriate language**
   - avoid swearing
   - use up-to-date, non-discriminatory terminology when referring to different groups

Visual aids

People take in up to three quarters of the information about their environment visually. They tend to remember things that they see more clearly than things that they hear.

Visual aids are therefore a very important component of an effective presentation. It is in your interest as a public speaker to use visual aids, to help your listeners' recollection of your talk, to break up the presentation and to create more interest.

Visual aids can be covered under eight main headings:

1. Yourself
2. General points
3. Handouts
4. The flip chart and whiteboards
5. The overhead projector
6. The visualizer
7. The slide projector
8. PowerPoint presentations

1. Yourself

It is vital to recognize that you are your own most important visual aid. How you look, move and control your body language will have a fundamental effect on the listeners' perception of you and your presentation.

Do not smoke, walk about too much or fiddle with pens, keys, small change, spectacles, paper clips or pointers. If you have to move, for example to get to a visual aid, look at the audience and talk as you walk, and they will hardly notice that you have changed your position. While focusing on your audience, concentrate for a few seconds on each person. Use positive gestures for emphasis, and try to look animated.

Clothes

The other item to concentrate on is what you plan to wear. When you stand up to give a public talk the audience very quickly assesses your appearance, and clothes play a large part in that.

There are no absolute rules about attire except that you should feel comfortable in the clothes you have chosen, and believe that they suit you and that you look smart and attractive in them.

If in doubt follow the four Cs:

Clean – shower or bathe, and wear clean clothes and shoes. If you are a man, ensure you shave or trim your beard/moustache neatly. If you are a woman, ensure that if you wear make-up it hasn't smudged.

Covered – make sure you do not have too much visible flesh on show, as it tends to reduce your credibility.

Checked – before your presentation make sure there are no loose buttons or zips, badly arranged clothing or smudges. It is a good idea to take with you a hairbrush, tissues and safety pins (for emergency repairs).

Comfortable – you should look smart but not at the expense of comfort. Avoid new shoes or heavy clanking jewellery that can become uncomfortable as the day wears on. The jewellery may also distract the audience from your message.

It is a good idea to dress like your listeners, and you should look at least as smart as the best-dressed person in your audience. If you dress like your audience it removes barriers. It is clearly your right to dress as you see fit. However, your audience does expect speakers to dress with a certain style; usually in clothes similar to their own. If you do decide to take a principled stand and go on to talk to your smartly dressed listeners in jeans and a tee shirt, you are likely to put an extra barrier between yourself and your audience. You will then have to work harder to overcome that barrier.

An experienced speaker and ex-athlete was seeking a significant charitable investment from bankers to provide sports facilities for underprivileged children. He had to give an open-air talk to a group of hopeful young sportspeople at an athletics field in the morning, and then give an afternoon presentation, in a boardroom, to a group of merchant bankers. He planned his strategy:

'I knew the kids were likely to relate better to me, and perhaps listen more carefully to what I had to say, if I was dressed like them and wore a tracksuit. On the other hand I was pretty certain that the bankers would not take me seriously if I turned up in anything other than a smart, pinstriped suit. Therefore I made sure I took a change of clothes with me and shed the tracksuit in favour of the pinstripe at lunchtime.'

When deciding what to wear, you should also consider the results of some research carried out in America.

Researchers at a well-known computer company discovered that speakers wearing plain, dark clothing were more likely to be believed, when saying the same thing and with similar body language, than those wearing light, pastel shades or heavily patterned items of dress.

This may have something to do with our respect for uniforms, but whatever the reason, it suggests that speakers should consider the advantage of wearing plain, dark clothes.

2. General points

- Try to get to the venue early, at least half an hour before the audience is due to arrive, so that you are able to check that the equipment is present and working. Run through your visual aids to ensure that they are in the correct order, that they are the right way up if they are photographic slides, and that any lettering, drawings and diagrams are clear and large enough to be seen from the back of the room.

- Make sure that boards or screens are placed so that everyone can see them: the corner of the room is best. Check the line of sight from various positions in the room. You must appreciate that you will be standing at the front and that you are not transparent, so you must stand away from the screen to ensure that the audience's view remains unobstructed.

- Try to keep visual aids simple. If the visual consists mainly of words, make the message as concise as possible. Use clear, easy-to-understand diagrams or photographs. Do not clutter your slides with any unnecessary material. The people at the back of the room will not be able to see the visual aid clearly and, while they are trying to interpret it, they will become annoyed and frustrated to the point that they will not be listening to what you say.

- Use colour for emphasis, but remember that colours like orange and yellow reflect light and are more difficult to see from a distance than blue or black. White is all right, but only against a dark background.

- Make sure that what you plan to illustrate is relevant. The points you emphasize with visuals will be the ones your audience remembers most clearly. They should be, at a minimum, the outline of the main points, the main points themselves and the summary. Remember that the summary slide should duplicate the outline slide.

- Do not display your visual aid before you need to refer to it or after you have finished with it; if you do, your audience's attention will remain on the visual aid instead of you.

- If you plan to show a film or video, make sure that you have seen it before you show it so that you know precisely what you want to get out of it. You might want to break up the viewing of a film, showing one section first, stopping the film, and showing the rest of it later. Many video or DVD players have display counters on which the numbers increase as the film progresses. Watch the film through and make a note of the numbers at the stopping points of your choice. When you come to show the film to an audience you can edit out sections of the film if you choose by fast-forwarding to the next appropriate number.

- Above all, always talk to your audience, not to your visual aids. It is important that, as you put on or change a slide, you look at the screen behind to make sure it is properly displayed, but ensure that the interval you take to look away from the audience is a brief one.

Many speakers use their slides as their notes and as a result spend long periods of their talks looking at the screen rather than their audience. In some cases speakers look at the screen because they find it far less threatening than all those faces looking at them. Audiences quickly pick up on this and realize, in most cases subconsciously, that a speaker is nervous.

To reiterate:

You must look at your audience while you are speaking to them.

You cannot do this if you are looking at your visual aid.

3. Handouts

Handouts are an extremely useful addition to your talk. They help your listeners follow the presentation and give them information that they can take away.

Keep the handouts concise. They should not include everything that you plan to say. If they do, you may as well give the handouts to the audience and then leave!

Always distribute handouts before you begin the main part of your talk. As well as helping the audience to follow the presentation, the handouts let the audience know what sort of notes they should take. It could be annoying when a speaker, whom the audience has been scribbling furiously to keep up with, says at the end of his or her talk, 'There is no need to take notes; I have a set of handouts.' Understandably, an audience much prefers to receive handouts at the beginning of a talk.

Speakers worry that if they give out the printed material in advance the audience will start to read it, and fail to pay attention to the talk. Clearly this might happen, but it is less likely to do so if you tell people that you are going to work through the handout and refer them to particular pages as the presentation continues. If they persist in reading do not worry, it is their choice and they will be receiving the information you have given them.

Do not give out important information while you are distributing the handouts or getting the audience to pass them round. People will not be paying attention as they are likely to be concentrating on the progress of the handouts.

4. The flip chart and whiteboards

The flip chart

This is simply a large pad of blank paper held upright on a metal stand but it is an extremely useful piece of equipment. You need no special training to use it, and because it does not require electricity it can be used anywhere.

- When using the flip chart face the audience and use your non-writing hand to grab the back of the stand. This will prevent you moving in front of the chart.

- Lightly pencil in headings or diagrams in advance. You can use the top corner of a flip chart for notes; if they are small no one will notice. Pre-preparation of charts and diagrams should be done in advance whenever possible, as it is time-consuming and boring to draw them up in front of the group. Try not to talk while you write as you will lose eye contact with your audience.

- To avoid the problem of turning over sheets of paper to find the one that you wish to display, cut a small corner off all the sheets preceding the one that you wish to show. All you need to do is feel along the corner of the cut sheets until you find, by touch, the first complete sheet. If you plan to display more than one sheet, use small Post-it notes on the appropriate pages of the pad. Both these techniques will give you quick access to your visual aid.

Whiteboards

These are shiny white surfaces usually fixed to the walls of the room. You can move them to different positions on the wall if they are fixed on metal runners.

- Use large flip-chart felt-tip pens to write on the boards. Be aware that a black barrel usually indicates that the pen is a permanent marker, which can only be removed with white spirit.

- Stand away from the board when you are showing it to the audience to ensure that people can see what you have written.

- On both flip charts and whiteboards use BIGGER letters than you think are necessary and space out ideas. Crowded, tiny writing is impossible to see from the back of an average-sized classroom or lecture theatre. Remember that cartoons or drawings add interest and make the visual aid easier to read.

5. The overhead projector

The use of the overhead projector, or OHP as it is often called, has become less common now as it is gradually replaced with PowerPoint. However, it is still found at many venues. It is a metal box containing a light, with a glass top and a mirror on a short vertical stand, which transfers the image from a slide placed on the glass to a screen. The mirror is held angled in a metal frame and the focus is adjusted by use of a knurled dial, which alters the position of the mirror either up or down the stand.

- Ensure that the electric flex is moved out of the way or safely taped down.

- The on/off switch is usually in a different place on each projector so carefully note where it is before you start.

- Do not stand in the line of sight of any members of the audience. It is a good idea to get to the room before your audience and sit in the positions that might have sighting problems, then you can work out your strategy for dealing with the issue.

- You will find that a blue or an orange border surrounds the image on the screen when the focus is changed. To bring the slide into focus, move the knurled dial until the mirror is between the positions in which the blue and orange border can be seen but neither border is now visible. The slide will now be roughly in focus and the dial can be carefully adjusted until perfect focus is achieved.

- The slide or small plastic sheet is known variously as a transparency, acetate or foil. It is preferable to print onto these, as this is easier to read than handwriting. However, if you have to handwrite due to time constraints, or because printing facilities are unavailable, use dark-coloured felt-tip pens such as blue or black. Reserve colours such as red or orange for bullet points or underlining.

- OHPs sometimes have acetate rolls attached. You can write or draw on these to illustrate points and take items from the group (during brainstorming, for example). Ensure that you write in large print and use a dark pen. Be careful not to smudge the writing as you move the acetate roll forward.

- Do not stand in front of the screen or use your hands to point to the screen. Use a pointer instead, or use your finger or pen to emphasize points on the acetate. Apart from being in the line of sight of some members of the audience as you stand next to the screen, pointing causes shadows to be thrown onto the screen, which is distracting for the audience. It is also possible that in this position you will find that the bright light of the overhead projector shines in your eyes, temporarily dazzling you.

6. The visualizer

This is a flat surface with attached lights that shine down onto the surface. It shows overhead-projector slides, solid objects, pages from books and the presenter writing in real time. The image is transposed to a screen via a data projector and can be magnified.

- Ensure the image is large enough, particularly if small print is being shown.

- When writing, print clearly using a dark pen; keep the writing to a minimum.

- Turn the visualizer off when you are not using it: you will not be able to use PowerPoint unless you do so.

7. The slide projector

Before you start:

- Check that the projector, the bulb, the focus and the remote control unit actually work.

- Number your slides and run through them to ensure they are in the correct order, clearly visible and not upside down or back to front. There are eight ways to load a slide – only one is correct.

- Bring blank slides with you to use at the beginning and end of the presentation and act as a buffer between sections of the talk.

- Check the room can be darkened effectively. If possible, arrange with an assistant beforehand to switch off the lights when requested to do so.

- If a projectionist is moving the slides for you, ensure that you have arranged a cuing system with him or her before you start.

- Laser pointers provide a light beam that throws a red dot onto the screen. They can be used to point to items on the slide (and can also be used with PowerPoint slides), but ensure that the pointer is held steadily and does not move around on the screen. Turn off the pointer as soon as you finish using it.

During the presentation:

- It is perhaps stating the obvious but do remember that you will lose eye contact in a dark room. It is therefore particularly important that you do not start the presentation in the dark. During the opening of a talk it is vital to make good eye contact with your audience. Although it might be tempting to create a situation in which they cannot see you, the result will be that you do not connect properly with your listeners and consequently they do not take in what you say. So start the talk with the lights on and only ask someone to switch them off when you are ready to show the slides. Switch the lights on again as soon as possible: it is not in your interest for the audience to fall asleep.

- Stand away from the equipment and the screen so that you do not obscure the audience's view. If possible use a remote control unit to change the slides.

- Keep visuals uncluttered. Use charts, graphs, diagrams and photographs, but not lots of words and figures. Use colour, unless the slides are old photographs and you have no choice; avoid black and white images that are difficult to see from the back of the room.

- Do not use too many images; turn the projector off when you are not using it.

- Remember that technical equipment tends to break down. Ensure that either you, or someone reliable, know how to make quick, basic repairs such as un-jamming slides or changing the projector bulb. If repairs do become necessary during your talk, spend only a short time on them or your audience will quickly become restless. You must therefore never rely completely on your slides, or indeed on any other visual aid: they should enhance your talk rather than replace your talk.

8. PowerPoint presentations

Microsoft PowerPoint is a powerful tool, which allows you to create and edit animated slide show presentations using a computer. The images are transposed, via a data projector, to the screen. It is usually unnecessary to darken the room for PowerPoint slides.

- After installing PowerPoint on your computer you can animate the slides by clicking the 'Slide Show' button on the toolbar and then the 'Custom Animation' button. You can make the slides appear in a variety of ways, from a number of positions on the screen and with or without sound. It is important not to use too much animation as it confuses your message and can irritate the viewers.

- Run through images to ensure they are in the correct order and clearly visible.

- Do not create too many slides and use them as your lecture notes. You will concentrate on the slides rather than your audience and lose eye contact with your listeners.

- Ensure the print fount is large enough – at least 24 point – for the slide to be read from the back of the room.

- Use a maximum of two fount styles per slide and keep the style consistent between slides. Only use italic (sloping) text sparingly for emphasis.

- Check the spelling on each slide.

VISUAL AIDS

- Keep slides uncluttered. It is often unnecessary to use words as well as pictures, as this crowds the slide. You can explain the symbols when you speak.

- Do not use contrived pictures that are there purely because they are the only ones you have in your small clip art collection.

- Do not mix graphical styles such as cartoons and photographs. Try not to use words or logos at different angles.

- If bullet points stretch over more than one line, put space between them to help them stand out as individual items.

- Ration bullet points – using too many is repetitive and can irritate your audience.

- Use the 'Custom Animation' button to animate slides, but remember not to overdo animation.

- Use a laser pointer where necessary (see 'The slide projector' above).

- The equipment will fail occasionally, so never be dependent on your slides.

Checklist

1. **Be aware of your own appearance and body language**
   - be clean and presentable
   - dress like your audience
   - do not move around too much

2. **Get to the venue early to check your visual aids**

3. **Make sure your visual aids are simple, relevant – and visible**

4. **Talk to your audience, not to your visual aids**

Questions

Asking questions

Asking questions of an audience is a useful tool. It promotes their participation, raises their interest levels and shows them that you are interested in what they think. It can help in clarifying their current level of knowledge and any possible gaps in it.

Questions can also monitor learning throughout the session and encourage people to put what they have learnt into words, which aids their recall of facts or ideas. Answering questions that you pose helps your audience to learn from each other and explore different approaches.

There are several different types of questions:

Open questions

Intended to start the other person talking about a topic, outline a situation, give a broad description of what happened and how he/she reacted.

These questions cannot be answered with a 'yes' or 'no'. The words 'what', 'why' and 'how' are good openers. For example:

> 'Tell me about ...?'
>
> 'What happened when ...?'
>
> 'I'd like to hear about ...'
>
> 'Why did that happen?'
>
> 'How did that occur?'

QUESTIONS

Probing questions

Used for getting to the nub of a topic, checking information or filling in detail. For example:

> *'Then what happened?'*
>
> *'How did you react ... ?'*
>
> *'What did you say exactly?'*

Closed questions

Used for establishing specific, single facts. They often invite a 'yes' or 'no' answer. For example:

> *'Did you do it?'*
>
> *'Who was it?'*
>
> *'How often?'*

Reflective questions

Used to help uncover feelings. For example:

> *'You say you were pleased ...?'*

Reflective probes

Used to gain more detail about what someone has said. For example:

> *'You say he reacted to this. How did he react?'*

Directed questions

These are put to individuals, often by name. They can be used to involve quieter members of the audience. However, you must be careful when using this technique and make an informed judgement on who you call on by name. Some people prefer to sit and quietly reflect on what they are being taught (see Part Three,

'The training seminar presentation'); others are nervous of speaking in public and should not be forced to do so.

Leading questions

These are not useful for obtaining value-free information.

> *'I suppose you took into account …?'*

Multiple questions

These can be confusing: the subject will usually answer the easiest or the last question. If they were all good questions they will have to be asked again, separately, so they waste time as well.

Answering questions

Allowing questions from the audience is a good idea as it helps them to feel involved and interested – similar feelings to those they experience when answering questions. They can also check their understanding or clear up a misleading point.

There are various issues for the speaker to consider, or techniques he or she can employ, when answering questions:

Timing

Decide before your talk if and when you are going to take questions and tell your audience. If you are an inexperienced presenter it may be better to take questions at the end of your talk. You could invite questions by saying:

> *'I'll be happy to answer your questions now.'*
>
> *'If you have any questions I'll be pleased to answer them now.'*
>
> *'We have some time now for questions and comments.'*

QUESTIONS

Taking questions can be nerve-racking. This is why members of parliament are normally allowed an undisturbed hearing during their maiden speech to the House of Commons. It is recognized that they will be nervous the first time they have to stand up and talk to the House. This polite convention allows them to settle and helps to give them the confidence to cope with the numerous interventions they will doubtless suffer later in their careers!

To a certain extent, questioning also turns over the timing of the session to your audience. You then have to be practised enough to regain control of the session without appearing to be too prescriptive.

Someone may dominate the question period and you have to ensure others get the opportunity of speaking (see Part Three, 'Chairing meetings', for techniques to help with this). The questioner may have strayed onto a topic which you are planning to cover later in your talk, or attempted to open a subject which is irrelevant to the one under discussion. You have to inform them of this and avoid the temptation to strike off at a tangent.

If you tell your audience that you will take questions at the end, then you know that your talk will take approximately the same amount of time it did in your practice sessions, and you are less likely to lose the thread of your thoughts if you are allowed to finish talking without interruption.

If you are used to public speaking, or if you feel confident enough to do so, it is better to tell the audience you are happy to take questions throughout your talk or, at least, at the end of each section of the presentation. This allows the questioners to quickly satisfy their curiosity and continue concentrating on the presentation. Moreover, if the talk is complex the listeners may need to check their understanding throughout to get the most from the experience.

Thanks

It is a polite gesture to thank your questioner for their question. You do not have to do so every time, but if the question is a good one, or allows you to open up a subject which might be helpful to other members of the audience, a simple thank you before you give the answer is justified and expected.

Plus, it gives you a little longer to think of the answer!

Restate or paraphrase the question

It is vital that you repeat or summarize each question for three reasons.

- Firstly, it ensures that you are about to answer the question that has actually been asked. The questioner has the opportunity to correct your understanding of their question or retract it and put another one.

- Secondly, if you repeat the question you ensure that all your listeners can hear the content, and avoid them witnessing a private interchange between the speaker and the questioner while they have no idea of what was asked.

- Thirdly, it also gives you a little longer to think of an answer!

Provide a straight answer

Avoid political tricks such as prevarication or avoidance. Typical examples include the classic 'That's an interesting question', closely followed by 'Before I answer let me say this' or 'That raises interesting issues ...'. The latter technique is an attempt to answer a completely different question.

If you know the answer, just say it. The straight answer may well include the admission, 'I don't know the answer to that question.'

Do not lie or make up a spurious answer: you will, sooner or later, be found out and your credibility will suffer.

Relay

This technique involves the speaker putting the question to the audience as a whole and asking them for their thoughts. This avoids a one-to-one discussion between a speaker and the questioner, and involves other audience members. It is particularly useful if one questioner is monopolizing the question period, because it often results in the discussion taking a different direction, and this allows other people to make a contribution.

Be careful not to use this technique too often or some members of the audience may think you are avoiding a question that you find difficult or impossible to answer.

Ricochet

Ricocheting the question is simply directing it to a named member of the audience, for example, 'I know Susan has done a considerable amount of work in this area and is probably better placed to answer this question than I am.'

However, it would be both polite and prudent to obtain your colleague's prior agreement to the proposition that she will take questions in her particular area of expertise.

Reverse

This technique involves throwing the question back to the questioner, for example:

> *'What do you think?'*

This can be used if you are unsure of your ground and you believe the questioner knows the answer and is testing you.

Clearly, it is not a technique that should be overused.

Peer pressure

This is used to check individual participants monopolizing time or the question period. You can say: 'I will try to come back to you but you have already asked a question and I am anxious to ensure as many people as possible have a chance to participate.' You then look away and take another question. If the questioner persists, which is unlikely but possible, the whole audience will be annoyed and someone else may ask him or her to give others a chance.

Do not:

- Use sarcasm or patronizing language to put down questioners.

- Spend any significant period arguing with questioners. Say something like: 'We'll have to agree to disagree' and move on.

Checklist

1. Decide before your talk if, and when, you will take questions

2. Thank the questioner for their question

3. Restate the question you have been asked
   - to make sure you are answering the intended question
   - so everyone has heard what has been asked
   - to give yourself more time to think of an answer

4. Do not use sarcasm, and do not force someone to speak if they do not want to

Timing

You must stick to the time agreed for your talk. If you fail to do so it is possible that you will inconvenience the event organizers, who, for example, may be desperate for the audience to be allowed to ask questions; your fellow speakers, who may be waiting for you to finish so they can speak; or the caterers, who may be waiting to serve lunch.

Most of all you are likely to annoy and frustrate the audience, with the result that they stop listening to you. If you overrun, some may even have to leave to fulfil other commitments.

You should also be aware that an intelligent adult audience will have an attention span of approximately 20 minutes. If you talk for much longer than 20 minutes, without asking or answering questions, setting the audience an exercise or giving them a break, you will lose the attention of your listeners, however interesting a speaker you are.

So it is very important that you finish your talk when you have agreed to do so, preferably in 20 minutes or less. How can you ensure this happens?

Use a clock

Do not rely on the teaching room to have a clock; even if it does there is a chance it will not work. Take a small, stand-alone, digital clock that displays minutes, and preferably seconds, and that you can see easily from a short distance away. Try not to use your wristwatch as the watch face is too small to see without difficulty. You will have to keep turning your arm to read it, which is very noticeable and off-putting for the audience. If you take it off and place it on the speaker's table, it will be even more difficult to read and will also mean that you have to look down, thereby losing eye contact with your audience.

If you have to use a wristwatch, alter the hands so that they will be approaching the hour, or half-hour, as your talk is due to finish. This trick will make it easier to read the watch from a short distance. But do remember to alter the hands back again after the talk is finished!

Use your finish time

Write down your finish time in large numbers, on a sheet of paper in front of you, as you stand up to begin your talk. You will find it impossible to do the mental arithmetic necessary to add, say, 15 minutes (the planned duration of your talk) to your start time of 10.37 when you are in the middle of your speech. If on the other hand you wrote down '10.52' as you started, it is relatively easy to judge your presentation in order to stop talking as your digital clock displays your finish time.

Practise

Practise your talk out loud before you have to give it in front of an audience. If possible, ask a friend or colleague to give you some informed, constructive criticism and adapt and change your talk as necessary. Time the final version carefully, but remember that you may talk more quickly in front of a real audience because of nerves. Try to slow down, and get used to the sound and rhythm of the phrases when the talk is given at the correct speed.

Practising the presentation is the only sure method of discovering how long it is likely to last.

Use cue cards

You can use your cue cards (see Part One, 'Use of cue cards') to help you stick to your time.

The key point to remember is to have 'essential', 'important' and 'nice to know' points from your talk scattered throughout the cue cards. You then underline each category in a different colour, for example, red for 'essential', blue for 'important' and green for 'nice to know'.

If you are running short of time and you come to a 'green' card, simply turn it over without mentioning the information it cues you to give. You can even do this with the 'blue' cards, but you *must* cover the information on the 'red' or 'essential' cards.

If you have lots of time you can include all the cards.

This is a particularly good technique to use if you are the last speaker in a group and the others have overrun into your scheduled time. It does no harm to point out at the start that you are now constrained for time so you will have to abbreviate your talk.

Checklist

1. Use a clock so you can check your time

2. Put a note of your planned finish time in front of you

3. Practise your presentation to discover how long it will last
    - ask a friend or colleague for constructive criticism
    - try to slow down

4. Use colour-coded cue cards
    - discard the non-essential points if you are running short of time

What to do if things go wrong

If you follow all the advice and instructions in this book it is unlikely that anything will go wrong, but even during the best prepared and managed presentations mishaps can occur. This section provides tips on what you can do if some of your worst fears actually start to come true.

You are held up on your journey to the venue

Strictly speaking this problem does not occur during the talk but this is the obvious place to refer to an issue that, unfortunately, is statistically extremely likely to occur to you if you do a large number of talks.

Always leave far more time for your journey than you think you will need, as it is usually less stressful that way. However, if there are problems such as traffic hold-ups, or train or plane delays, try to contact the venue as soon as you realize you are going to be late.

There are few things in life more frustrating than trying to get a number from directory inquiries when you are under stress. The answer is to take the relevant number and contact name with you. If you have a mobile phone, store the name and number of your contact person at the venue in your phone, before you leave your office or home for your speaking engagement. Take your phone with you and ensure the battery is charged.

If, after repeated attempts, you are unable to speak to somebody, you may as well relax as there is little you can do. Panicking will not help and you could try reassuring yourself with the idea that the person concerned and all your potential audience are probably caught up in the same travel nightmare as you are.

The only useful action you can perform, assuming you are not driving, is to look at your notes or cue cards and try to work out what you can cut out to fit the almost inevitable reduction in the time you now have available to speak.

Your visual aids do not work

This might be because the equipment that you have carefully ordered, in writing and in advance, is for some inexplicable reason not present.

It could be because although the equipment is there you cannot get it to work. For example, the laptop computer is incompatible with the memory stick you have brought containing your PowerPoint presentation, or the connection to the data projector does not appear to be working.

The equipment might have failed – the bulb is not working, for instance – and no replacements are available.

You can be sure that technical equipment, particularly computers, will at some point let you down. Therefore, take at least one hard copy of your PowerPoint or overhead projector slides with you. If the worst comes to the worst it can be copied for the participants: even better, request copies from the organizers in advance.

However, your best safeguard is to ensure that your presentation does not rely on visual aids, and that you are able to give your talk without them if necessary.

Some of the audience have more/less knowledge of the subject than you were led to believe

If this is true for all the audience, and all of them have the same level of knowledge, you should adjust your talk if it is possible for you to do so at short notice.

However, it is more usually the case that only a few members of the audience are going to find the level of the talk too simple or too complex. In this case you should talk to them before your presentation if possible and explain the situation. Allow them to decide whether they wish to stay.

It is probable, and certainly desirable, that the details of your talk were publicized beforehand. It is important you keep to the published details as the majority of your audience will have decided to attend on that basis. If you try to adapt the talk for the minority, most of your audience may feel understandably annoyed.

You lose your place, or concentration, and 'dry up'

Firstly, remember that what feels like a long silence to you is probably not even going to be noticeable to the audience unless you draw attention to the problem.

Concentrate on your audience. Do not to look at the ceiling, the floor or the screen. You will lose eye contact with the listeners and allow them to realize what has happened. Their resultant tension, and possibly embarrassment, will make things worse for you.

The panic of forgetting your words or losing your thread is often worse than the event itself. If you worry about this particular negative before your presentation it makes it more likely that it will occur.

It is not a good idea to learn your talk by heart. Clearly you should know it well and have practised it out loud, but if you learn it by rote you will fail to engage with your audience or with what you are actually saying. You will talk on 'automatic pilot' and the slightest thing could throw you off your stride and contribute to you losing your place.

If you use cue cards and practise using them, you should find that after a while you turn them over when you make a point. Read the next card, think for a second and your words will come back to you.

If you do forget what you were saying and are taking a long time to remember what you were about to say, take a deep breath. Look at the audience and smile. This releases their tension and will probably help you. This may do the trick and your words will then return from the ether. If not, be honest, say something like:

> *'I've lost my place – now what was I going to tell you?'*

Look at the audience while you say this. Providing you have adequately prepared your talk, the resultant decrease in tension for yourself and the audience will allow you to pick up the thread of your presentation.

Members of the audience are falling asleep

Say, 'It is getting stuffy in here' and, if you can, open some windows. If you have an audience participation exercise you can set them, do so. The other alternative is to ask them to stand up if they have done or felt something in connection with your subject. For example:

> *'Stand up if you have ever claimed any sort of government benefit.'*

'Stand up if you have a family member that has ever received a government benefit.'

'Stand up if you know someone who has ever received a government benefit.'

'Stand up if you have ever received mortgage tax relief.'

'If you aren't already standing up – do so. I think we all need a stretch!'

Members of the audience are chatting

Do not automatically assume this is a bad thing. Audiences talk for a host of reasons. They may be borrowing a pen or paper, or checking understanding, or be so fascinated by what you are saying they cannot wait to discuss it.

With adult audiences it is usually enough to fall silent for a moment. The talkers will realize they are disturbing others and be quiet. If this does not work, try looking at them silently, and if necessary ask them if they are talking about something they feel they should share with the rest of the group.

Remain even-toned and polite and this does not need to be a problem.

Hecklers

Hecklers disagree with what you are saying, may aggressively interrupt you and can even be personally offensive.

Fortunately, hecklers are unlikely in adult audiences, unless you are making a political speech or talking on a subject about which people have strong views. If you get heckled, remain outwardly composed. Even if you feel upset or angry, try not to show it.

WHAT TO DO IF THINGS GO WRONG

The first step is to fall silent for a moment and look at the person or people concerned.

If that does not work, the next stage is to try to find some merit in their argument, express agreement with that issue, break eye contact and move on.

> 'No we do not agree on points X and Y, but nevertheless we can agree on points A and B.'

Alternatively, wait for some misstatement of fact and throw it out to the audience for correction. Failing that, calmly correct the person yourself.

If none of this works you may need to use one or more of the following phrases:

> 'I see your viewpoint; now please consider mine.'

> 'I appreciate the reasons for your anger, but there is another side to the story, to which I hope you and rest of the audience will give your consideration.'

> 'You set out your case with eloquence and passion. It is now only courteous to allow me to do the same.'

> 'We may disagree but we are all here for a common purpose. Personal abuse will not help us achieve that purpose which is ... [state purpose].'

> 'I appreciate your frankness but I do not accept your insinuations. If we could now look at the situation calmly ...'

> 'I am sorry you have chosen to deal with such a serious and complex matter in such an aggressive way. I feel it would help if we tried to examine the issue objectively.'

This is obviously a difficult, but thankfully rare, situation. Take heart – usually your audience will be on your side. As a final tactic try this:

> *'It is impossible to continue with these interruptions –*
> *perhaps we can take a break until feelings cool down.*
> *We will start again in 15 minutes.'*

Hope that the organizers or other audience members deal with the hecklers during the break. If, when you continue, things are as bad as before, you may have to bow out gracefully – apologizing to those people, who will probably be in the majority, who did want to hear you.

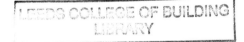

Part Three

Types of Presentation

Room layouts

The room layout you choose is dependent on the type of session you are running.

Here are some regularly used layouts:

- Open U style with tables
- Open horseshoe style
- Boardroom style
- Open square
- Theatre style
- Classroom style
- Herringbone

Each layout has merits and disadvantages.

Open U style with tables

This type of layout is often used for training seminars.

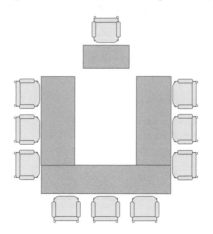

Advantages

- All the participants can see each other and are therefore more likely to interact.
- They have a place to put their papers and can easily make notes.
- The speaker can move into the middle of the open U if desired.

Disadvantages

- The layout takes up a lot of space and if space is limited people may find it difficult to get out, or stretch their legs if table legs hamper them.
- Open U is not so suitable for large numbers. Apart from taking up too much space, it means that people at the top and the bottom of the long sides of the U will find it difficult to see each other.

Open horseshoe style

This layout is also used in training seminars, particularly in those where there is likely to be a lot of intense discussion.

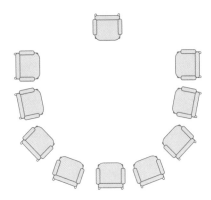

Advantages

- All the participants can see each other.
- The layout makes interaction far more likely. There are no barriers, in the form of tables, between the participants nor between the participants and the speaker or facilitator (that is, somebody who, rather than lecturing to a group, facilitates discussion and decisions).

Disadvantages

- Some participants may feel intimidated by the lack of barriers between themselves and the other participants and/or the facilitator.
- There isn't anywhere for people to write or to put papers.
- The layout is difficult to use for large audiences (although the horseshoe can be extended to form a circle).

Boardroom style

This layout is often used for meetings, and it can also be used for training events.

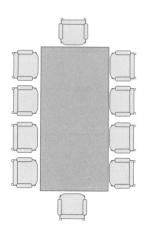

Advantages

- All the participants can see each other.
- They have a place to put their papers and can easily make notes.

Disadvantages

- It is an inflexible layout as the speaker or chairperson is seated at one end of the table and cannot move closer to the participants at the other end.
- The people at either end of the long sides of the table cannot see each other easily. Boardroom style cannot work with large numbers of participants.

Open square

This layout is commonly used for large meetings.

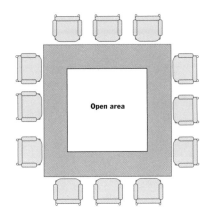

Advantages

- All the participants can easily see each other.
- They have a place to put their papers and can make notes without problems.

Disadvantages

- It is an inflexible layout.
- It is extremely difficult to use visual aids as some of the participants will always have their backs to the screen.
- To get into the middle of the square, to adjust a visual aid or recording device, someone has to climb over or under the tables.

Theatre style

This layout is used at training seminars, but more often at larger conferences.

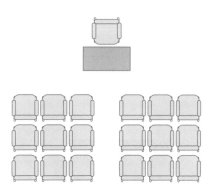

Advantages

- This layout enables the greatest number of people to be fitted into the available space.

Disadvantages

- Participants cannot see each other unless they are sitting side by side.
- There is nowhere for people to write or to put papers.

Classroom style

This layout is used at training seminars, but more often at larger conferences which require facilities for participants to make notes in more comfort than ordinary theatre style.

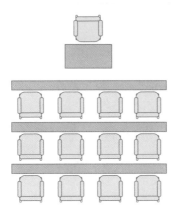

Advantages

- Allows the largest possible number of people to sit with writing facilities.

Disadvantages

- Takes up more space than theatre style.

Herringbone

This layout is also used for conferences; herringbone can be used in a classroom style to provide writing facilities.

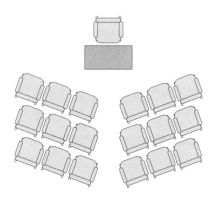

Advantages

• Although people are sitting in rows, a herringbone layout does allow more people to see one another and so it feels friendlier.

Disadvantages

• Takes more space than theatre style.

It is important that you choose the room layout that best suits the type of presentation that you are planning to make.

The training seminar presentation

To run an effective training event you have to be aware of how different people learn.

Learners can be classified under four headings:

- Activists
- Reflectors
- Theorists
- Pragmatists

Activists

Activists are always keen to seek challenges. You can expect them to be gregarious, impetuous, impatient, untroubled at the thought of getting something wrong, open-minded and flexible. These are people who will not baulk at being asked to do something new or outside their normal routine.

Reflectors

Reflectors tend to be cautious, methodical and thoughtful. They 'stand back', gather data, ponder and analyse. They often have intelligent insights about their work and are capable of criticizing themselves constructively. They are good at listening to others and will rarely jump to conclusions.

Theorists

Theorists tend to be rational and objective, and think things through in logical steps. They are disciplined in their approach to learning, assimilate disparate facts into coherent theories and reject subjectivity and flippancy.

Pragmatists

Pragmatists seek and try out new ideas. They are practical and down-to-earth; they enjoy problem-solving and speedy decision-making. They get bored with long discussions.

Learning styles

When learning, activists and pragmatists tend to prefer a 'student-centred' approach with case studies, exercises and quizzes. However, pragmatists will quickly get bored if group discussions go on for too long.

Reflectors and theorists are likely to prefer lectures, providing they are well delivered and logical. Theorists, in particular, will need to see that any exercises or case studies are relevant and have a logical outcome.

In your audiences there will be a mix of different types of people. An effective training event therefore needs to employ a mix of training techniques to appeal to the widest range possible.

Promoting participation

Promoting participation in an audience during training sessions is extremely important as it aids their understanding of the subject. Bear in mind the well-known saying:

> *What I hear, I forget.*
>
> *What I see, I remember.*
>
> *What I do, I understand.*

Promoting participation can be done with the audience as a whole by using methods such as:

- starting a question-and-answer session
- brainstorming
- conducting a survey or voting
- quizzes
- Post-it notes (people respond to problems posed on notes stuck on walls or whiteboards)

Group training to promote participation is now extremely common. The groups can be created by various methods:

- putting people who work together in the same group
- asking them to form their own groups of a particular number of people (beware of this, as it usually results in a short period of chaos with some people being left out)
- numbering people sitting together, from 1 up to an appropriate number (try not to go above 6), then starting a new group when you reach the chosen number
- counting people off, telling them to remember their number then putting all the 'ones' together, all the 'twos' together and so on

Use different methods throughout the course so that people are not always working in the same groups, and so are exposed to different points of view and different problems of interaction. Using groups means that you can pose different problems.

These include:
- Case study
- Exercises
- Role-play

THE TRAINING SEMINAR PRESENTATION

Case study

The group is confronted with a situation, drawn from real life or invented, which they have to solve using skills they have already been taught or are about to be taught. Sometimes they pick up the necessary skills themselves by working through the case study. The trainer simply has to get them to identify the skills they have employed. Often there is no completely right or wrong answer. Case studies are best employed to try to help groups find answers to problems involving people.

Exercises

This is similar to the case study except that the group is asked to solve an abstract problem, which usually has one correct answer and does not involve recounting experiences. For example, a group may be given a list of various tasks associated with administrative work in an office and be asked to prioritize the tasks in the correct order in which they should be carried out.

Role-play

This involves a small group, perhaps with two people acting out either side of a problem, plus one observer. Role-plays are often used to help people practise particular behaviours.

Instructing groups

You must give all the participants clear instructions before they carry out their task:

- Separate them into groups.

- Tell them where the groups should sit (if this involves some of the groups having to go to a different room, ask them to wait until they have received their instructions).

- If appropriate, tell them that their first task will be to choose a recorder/spokesperson – these may be two separate people. Hand out flip-chart paper, or Post-it notes, and pens for them to record their discussions.

- Tell them how long they have to complete the task, where they should congregate when the task is completed and what is going to happen at completion (feedback, handing in answers, etc).

- Distribute handouts with the task printed on them; ensure there are enough copies for everyone.

- Make sure that everyone is clear about what they have to do!

While the groups are working, the trainer should circulate, checking understanding, answering questions (without performing the task for them) and reminding the groups of the time.

Checklist

1. Use a mix of training techniques to appeal to different learning styles

2. Promote participation in your audience

3. If you have given people a problem to solve, give them clear instructions

The large conference presentation

Large conference presentations can be intimidating. You have many people looking at you waiting for you to speak. It is important you see this as an opportunity to put across your views, your work or your beliefs in as positive a manner as possible.

Before the talk

If a fee is payable, agree the fee and the payment arrangements in advance, in writing.

It is normal practice to send a synopsis of your talk, or even a comprehensive paper, to the conference organizers some weeks before the event. In addition, you will probably be sent a questionnaire to complete which inquires about your visual aids, handouts, accommodation and meal requirements. Make sure you return this in good time! If no such sheet is forthcoming, write or e-mail the organizers with your requirements. Request a reply so that you know they have received your communication. If you receive no reply, follow up your original request with a further letter, e-mail or phone call.

Be polite but assertive in your requests. Do not worry about making a nuisance of yourself: these issues are part of the organizers' job. Remember it is you, not they, who will look unprofessional in front of a large audience if the audiovisual equipment or handouts you require are not in place on the day.

It is likely that you will be expected to speak from a stage, perhaps from behind a lectern. There will probably be a separate speakers' table, a short distance from the lectern, at which the chairperson and speakers will sit. You are likely to be introduced, by the chairperson, from the speakers' table just before, or during, your walk to the lectern. You return to the table after your speech.

You will almost certainly be expected to use the microphone provided to amplify your voice.

Ensure that you do the following:

- Ask if it is possible to meet any other speakers and the chairperson beforehand to finalize the details of the session.

- Speak to the chairperson to clarify any biographical details, the pronunciation of your name and how you are to be introduced.

- If possible, visit the room in which you will be speaking before your talk.

- Check if the stage or platform layout is to your liking. If not, is it possible to change the layout? Remember that other speakers may be involved and a compromise may be necessary.

- If the microphone is fixed, check that it is at the correct height for you. If not, can it be easily changed before you speak?

- If you need to move around the stage, ask if it is possible to get a lapel microphone that fixes to your clothes, or a radio or wireless microphone that you can carry with you.

- Check that your slides can be seen from the back of the room. If not, and you have time, change your slides. This is relatively easy to do with PowerPoint by increasing the fount size on each slide. Remember this may necessitate increasing the number of slides. If the slide cannot be seen, and you are unable to change it, do not use it.

- Check if the visual-aid equipment is easy to reach, or if there is a remote control mechanism for changing slides. If so, how does it work?

- If a technician changes the slides, find out how you communicate with him or her.

- Check if there is a laser pointer and, if so, that it works.

- Check if there will be water available in case your mouth becomes dry.

- Just before you are due onstage, go to the bathroom, and check your appearance and your clothes for loose or unfastened buttons or zippers, smudges and fluff. Ensure you have any notes or cue cards and timing devices to hand. Focus your thoughts on your audience and on how you are about to deliver your speech to provide them with a memorable experience.

During the talk

- Look at your audience. Using the five-person trick (first mentioned in Part Two, 'Body language'), choose a person at the extreme right of the front row and a person at the extreme left of the front row. Next, choose a person at either end of the back row. You should now have picked a person in each corner of the audience. Choose a person in the centre of the audience. Finally, move your eyes regularly from person to person, among your chosen five people, ensuring you do so at eye-level height. You will have to move your head to do this. If you follow this technique, every member of the audience will feel you are looking at them.

- Ensure that, if you are using a fixed microphone, you do not talk as you turn away, to check on your slides for example. If you talk while turning your head away from the microphone your voice will not be amplified and most of the audience will not hear what you say.

- Use the laser pointer if there is one, but while using it hold it in both hands to prevent the dot on the screen shaking or creating intricate patterns. Turn off the laser pointer quickly. Remember that while you are using the pointer you will be looking at the slide and turning away from any fixed microphone, so explain what you are going to show the audience in advance. Only start speaking again when you have turned back to the microphone.

- If you want to encourage interaction during your conference speech you can use a technique known as 'buzz groups'. Buzz groups are named after the hubbub created by small groups of people engaged in discussions. They should not be used merely to revive attention, but to engage your audience in thought as well as discussion. Buzz groups involve asking your listeners to tackle a small task in pairs or in threes. They will normally be sitting next to someone they know so there is usually no problem in getting them to talk to one another. It is almost impossible for even the most reticent people to stay silent in these circumstances. Your audience needs to appreciate the purpose of using buzz groups. They require clear instructions on what to do, how long to do it and what is expected from them at the end. These instructions must be on a slide, as well as given verbally. However, you should use buzz groups with discretion, and it is probably wise to employ the technique only once during your speech.

- Ensure that you stick to your allotted time. This is particularly important if you are to be followed by other speakers. Take a small digital clock with you and follow the guidelines given in Part Two, 'Timing'.

After the talk

The chairperson will probably chair a question period, and it is likely that the audience will be encouraged to use a radio microphone to put their questions, in order that the chairperson, speakers and the rest of the audience can hear them. If this is the case, there is no overriding need to repeat the question unless you wish to check your understanding of what the questioner was saying. If you can provide a straight answer do so, otherwise follow the techniques outlined in Part Two, 'Answering questions'.

Try to learn from each conference presentation, indeed each presentation of any sort, that you give. Ask the chairperson, organizers and perhaps even your fellow speakers for honest feedback. Some conferences provide the audience with evaluation forms. You should receive the results from your session later in summary form. Study such information carefully; try to extract any lessons that you can put to good use in subsequent conference speeches.

Checklist

1. **Before the talk**
- Send the organizers a synopsis of your talk
- Let the organizers know your requirements
- If possible, visit the room in which you will be speaking

2. **During the talk**
- look at your audience
- encourage interaction if you wish
- stick to your allotted time

3. **After the talk**
- follow the techniques outlined in Part Two for answering questions

Chairing meetings

Role of the chairperson

It is the chairperson's job to ensure that the meeting is run in a structured way that meets the objectives, and gives an equal opportunity for all to contribute rather than one or two forceful characters.

Five basic questions

If you are chairing a meeting or a session at a conference you need to consider the following questions – the five Ws. You will note that the order and the details are slightly different to the five Ws that you use for talks, as outlined in Part One, 'The five Ws':

- Why is the meeting/session taking place?
- When will it be held?
- Where will it be held?
- Who will be attending?
- What is going to be covered?

Why

Firstly, is the meeting or session necessary? Define the purpose, why it is taking place and what should happen as a result.

When

Clarify the date and start/finish time. Ensure that the meeting participants or the people attending the sessions are informed of the date and times well in advance.

Where

Get clear directions for the venue and let people know where it is. Get information about the room, how large it is, how it will be laid out and the equipment available.

Who

Analyse the participants: their number, level of knowledge or expertise, and the issues they want to cover. Ensure you have a secretary; you cannot chair and take minutes.

What

If you are chairing a standard meeting, compile an agenda by using issues raised by the participants (ask for items well in advance of the meeting), or construct your own agenda as chairperson, or use a combination of both. Formal agendas should start with:

- apologies
- minutes of last meeting
- matters arising from minutes
- new issues (put important or controversial items in the middle of the agenda, less important issues towards the end)
- any other business
- date and location of next meeting

Ensure that the agenda, together with the relevant papers, location map and start/finish time, are sent out a minimum of two weeks beforehand if the participants already have the meeting booked (if not, they should be contacted a minimum of two months beforehand to secure the time in their diaries).

Make sure that you read the papers and do your research on each agenda item before the meeting.

The chairperson's tasks

The meeting chairperson has five main tasks:

1. Opening the meeting
2. Controlling the meeting
3. Summarizing discussions
4. Dealing with problems
5. Following up the meeting

1. Opening the meeting

Dress like the other people at the meeting and check your appearance before the start of the meeting.

It helps to arrive early, take your place and lay out your papers. It ensures that participants are coming onto your territory, not vice versa, and that you look unflustered.

Start the meeting on time; do not wait for late arrivals. You need to show you are in charge without appearing bossy or dictatorial. It is important that the people who are punctual do not sit and wait, otherwise at the next meeting even fewer people will be on time.

Look at them, smile, introduce yourself and welcome them to the meeting. Thank them for coming. Welcome new participants. If numbers attending do not preclude it, get everyone to introduce him or herself. Refer them to the agenda and check all items are still relevant. Ask if there are particularly urgent items that should be added to any other business: if there are, you may have to miss out a non-urgent item or extend the meeting by an agreed amount of time.

Take apologies for absence and introduce the first item.

2. Controlling the meeting

Never forget that you are in charge. Steer people forward, keeping to the agenda at all times. Introduce each item and encourage participants to speak. Allow time for clarification of difficult items. As each item is finished, summarize what has been said. Keep an eye on the time; if an item is taking too long, try to bring discussion to a close politely but firmly. Give praise where it is due: if a participant has been helpful then say so. You are there to give positive backing rather than finding fault.

Keep it simple and straightforward

Try to make people feel more comfortable and less inhibited. Never use a big word where a small one will do. People much prefer to understand what you are talking about. Use 'we' or 'you' rather than 'I'. Keep your sentences short. Avoid formal terms such as 'point of order'.

Keep it relevant

Follow through the agenda in a logical order. Try to ensure that the important points occur in the middle of the agenda. Spend longer on the important or controversial items; do not allow the meeting to spend the majority of time on trivia.

Stop people going off at tangents by explaining that essentials must be dealt with first. If there is time their topic can be covered under any other business at the end of the meeting. In reality, there will rarely be time but a harsh dismissal of a person's views will not help efficient meeting management.

All opinions should be respected and everyone's area of expertise should be utilized. That is one of the reasons for calling a meeting in the first place: to get an interaction of ideas.

People behave differently in groups than they do individually.

Everyone has to speak in front of his or her peers and conflicts of ideas are inevitable. Some people find public speaking like this intimidating.

Use appropriate body language

Eye contact is the most important aspect of body language. As chairperson you need to look at people to check their understanding and whether they are trying to attract your attention. Spend a few seconds on each person; do not concentrate on one or two friendly faces. Smile!

Show interest and commitment to the aims of the meeting. Listen to what is being said and show that you are listening: use head nods, and an animated expression. Do not overuse gestures such as throwing your arms around to emphasize important points or banging your fists on the table.

Interpreting signals from others

Eye contact

People who look at you are likely to be listening to what you say.

Body direction

In a normal meeting people sit facing the chairperson. If someone turns their body away they may not be impressed with what is happening.

Head movements

People can unconsciously show their agreement or otherwise by nodding or shaking their head.

Facial expressions

People's expressions are usually a reasonably accurate guide to their feelings. They can try to disguise their emotions but they find this difficult to sustain and continue to look natural.

Hand movements
Movements of the hand near the mouth usually indicate people are uncomfortable with what they are saying or may even be lying. Arms folded can indicate defensiveness; hand-wringing or nail-biting can betray nervousness.

3. Summarizing discussions

Summarize each item as the meeting progresses. Decisions are usually reached by group discussion, although votes may be taken when agreement cannot be reached. Allow time for everybody to express their views, then give your own. Try to summarize the arguments for and against. Get someone to make a proposal or make one from the chair, and take a vote. You or the minute-taker should note the result.

4. Dealing with problems

The latecomer
Late arrivals are disturbing, but assume the reason is genuine and accept the apology if offered. If someone consistently arrives late and the lateness is avoidable, then different treatment is merited.

On the first occasion give a brief summary of proceedings. However, if you do this every time you may make the latecomer feel there is no need to make an effort to be on time. Next time try looking pointedly at the clock, halting the meeting entirely until they have sat down, and continuing without a summary. This should embarrass them into better timekeeping. Otherwise take them to one side after the meeting and explain that the situation is disruptive and cannot continue.

The early leaver

Assuming that you know the person is going to be leaving early, and they do not do this regularly, try to finish the main business before they have to leave. You may change the order of the agenda so the item(s) that concern them are dealt with earlier.

The silent type

This is the person who says nothing when you need them to speak. They are usually shy or unsure. Use their first name and tell them that everyone else would value their input.

The chatterbox

If someone is talking to a neighbour try silently looking at them. If this does not work quickly then ask, 'Was there something you wanted to say? I couldn't quite hear you.'

If this person talks too much in the meeting wait for them to draw breath, summarize what they have said in a sentence and quickly move on to the next person. If it continues, say firmly, 'Thanks, John, but I want to ensure that other people contribute' and turn expectantly to the meeting. Continually ask for other contributions – if no one responds they clearly do not mind this person dominating their meeting.

The confused

This is the person who does not appear to understand what is going on and continually asks questions, thus holding up proceedings and exasperating others. You should summarize each item in the simplest possible terms. If there is still a problem you can suggest they come to see you at the end for further explanations.

The 'expert'

This person talks on any subject at great length. Faced with such a person, you can use the chatterbox technique above. If they are

123

wrong, try to give them a face-saving way out, for example, 'You may not have had a chance to read the latest paper on this.' You do not want to get embroiled in an argument.

The plotter
This person is either trying to block or push through an item, working to a hidden agenda. Try to draw them out by exposing them; you might ask, 'I don't understand why you're against this Jane. Could you explain?' Once the reasons for blocking or pushing have been explained, throw the item open to the meeting. Use peer pressure to control the person.

The aggressor
This person makes rude or personal remarks. Stop this immediately. Say, 'You might not agree with Sue but can we please discuss the matter without the personal remarks?' By retaliating before the person who is the focus of the remarks does so, you should defuse the situation. If they interrupt a colleague you could say, 'Perhaps you could tell us your views when Arun has finished, as he might resolve the problem for us if he is allowed to continue.'

The complainer
This is the person who continually finds fault. Listen to them, check understanding and then challenge them. Explain that matters under discussion need to be resolved and that all comments must be restricted to this. You can listen and then ask if the rest of the meeting agrees, but this is a risky strategy: it should only be tried if you think the complainer is in a minority, or if you are prepared to do something about a justified complaint.

5. Following up the meeting
Was the meeting a success? Ask yourself the following questions:

- Were the venue, room layout, equipment and refreshments satisfactory?
- Did the meeting start and finish on time?
- Were the correct people in attendance?
- Was the agenda followed?
- Were accurate minutes taken?
- Did the meeting fulfil its objectives?

Any negative answers need to be investigated and corrected.

Implementing decisions

Implementing decisions is one of the biggest problems arising from a meeting. It helps to take accurate notes, with proper 'action points' identifying who should do what, but some chivvying by the chairperson may also be necessary. A failure to act on decisions lowers the morale of all, even though only one or two may be at fault. It needs to be pointed out that the success of the meeting rests with everyone. Meetings are pointless unless something actually happens as a result.

Sending correspondence

It is important that copies of minutes are sent out as soon as possible. A letter gently drawing people's attention to the action points may accompany this. If it is necessary to send other papers, ensure that it is clear to which agenda points these are related. Explain them further if necessary.

Assessing your performance

Ask yourself:

- Was I well prepared?
- Did I dress appropriately?
- Did I show the right attitude and body language?

- Did I dominate the meeting too much?
- Did everyone get a chance to put their views forward?
- Did I summarize effectively?
- Did I deal effectively with problem people?

It is a good idea to ask other people at the meeting for feedback; you may even use a questionnaire. Participants can often come up with ideas for improvements you had not thought of.

If you did well, congratulate yourself and enjoy your success!

Chairing conference sessions

If you are chairing a conference session, here is a list of points to consider:

- What is the session going to cover? Ensure you have short biographies of the speakers you are to introduce, the duration of each speech, the order in which they will speak and the detail of the topics to be covered.

- Talk to the speakers before the session. Check the pronunciation of any difficult names and that the information you have on each of them is correct. Ask how they would like to be introduced. (A famous female speaker was once introduced as the wife of her even more famous husband. She was obviously, and understandably, annoyed.)

  Reinforce messages about the timing of both their talk and the session as a whole.

- Introduce each speaker in turn, and after each has finished start the applause and thank him or her before introducing the next person.

  It is usually better to take questions from the floor after all the speakers have finished; if you allow questions between speakers it can badly affect the timing of the session. It is also possible that questions will stray onto the topics to be covered in later talks.

- Try to choose questioners from all parts of the room and from a wide cross-section of the audience. Do not allow individuals to dominate proceedings or stray too far from the subject under discussion. Ask the questioners to identify themselves and, in large venues, encourage them to use microphones to ensure they are heard. The microphones should be placed around the room or be brought to questioners by attendants.

- After the question period thank all the questioners and ask the audience to again thank the speakers. Make any relevant announcements and close the session.

Informal presentations

Informal presentations or speeches may be given at occasions such as sports or social gatherings, leaving or retirement parties, or after meals.

The primary purpose of informal presentations is to entertain rather than inform the audience, and if they do both, that is a bonus.

Nevertheless, for informal presentations you are still required to follow most of the rules applied to other talks. Arrive in good time, avoid alcohol before your talk, dress with the same degree of smartness or casualness as your listeners and find out as much as you can about the audience and the event.

Structure your speech. Making an impact at the opening of this sort of talk is very important, as is an impact at the end. It is perhaps not so vital to worry about the outline, or interim summing-up, as it would be in a technical talk or training presentation, but if you include them many people will find the talk easier to follow and therefore more enjoyable.

Good body language is crucial. As always, remember to look at the audience, use calm measured hand gestures and do not move about too much.

Humour

Humour is often an essential ingredient of informal talks. However, you must ensure that you do not offend your audience.

Racist and sexist 'jokes' or so-called humour about people with disabilities are in thoroughly bad taste and likely to alienate your audience. Steer well clear of any anecdotes in this vein.

Given the proviso above, do use humour. An audience loves it. The commonest comic structure is the 'set-up', followed by the 'punchline'.

The set-up may not in itself be amusing. It is the clear, simple information that comes before the punchline.

The punchline is delivered as if it is a spontaneous comment on the information you have just been giving the audience in the set-up. It could be visual, ie something the audience can see. It can be as mad, exaggerated or sarcastic as you feel you can get away with.

Place the jokes throughout the presentation, and make your delivery natural. Do not labour the funny lines or laugh at your own witty remarks: try for a conversational style, with no partic- ular emphasis on the joke. You are more likely to get a laugh if you do this, but if you do not it is easy to continue with no sign that you are discomfited.

If you are lucky enough to make your audience laugh, then stop speaking to allow them to do so.

If you follow the rules, put in the preparation, do the practising and believe in yourself, you'll find informal presentations – in fact, any presentation – can be fun.

As unlikely as it may seem to you at the moment, you can get to the point when you enjoy speaking in public.

Checklist

1. **Follow most of the rules applied to more formal talks**
- arrive in good time
- avoid alcohol before your talk
- dress like your audience

2. **Structure your talk to some degree**
- make an impact at the opening and at the end

3. **Be aware of your body language**
- look at your audience
- do not move around too much

4. **Use humour, but ensure you do not offend your audience**

Index

Index

INDEX